THE INDEPE
GUIDE
DISNEYLAND
PARIS 2022

G. COSTA

Limit of Liability and Disclaimer of Warranty:
The publisher and the author have used their best efforts in preparing this book, and the information provided herein is provided "as is." Independent Guides and the author make no representation or warranties with respect to the accuracy or completeness of the contents of this book and specifically disclaims any implied warranties of merchantability or fitness for any particular purpose and shall in no event be liable for any loss of profit or any other commercial damage, including but not limited to special, incidental, consequential, or other damages. Please read all signs before entering attractions, as well as the terms and conditions of any third party companies used. Prices are approximate, and do fluctuate.

COVID-19 RELATED UPDATES

At the time of writing, the world is going through a pandemic. Several changes have been made to Disneyland Paris to ensure the safety of guests. This book was written to be relevant before, during and after Covid-19.

As we don't know how long the pandemic will last, we have not rewritten every section as we want this book to be useful for future visits too. You should be aware that the following changes may apply during your visit. These changes are up to date as of early January 2022 but may change in the coming months.

Wearing a mask is compulsory for all visitors six years of age and over (except during meals), Cast Members (staff) and service providers.

In line with French authorities' latest requirements, a Health Pass is required for any guests aged above 12 years and 2 months in order to visit the Disney Parks, the Disney Hotels and Disney Village. You can present this digitally on the 'TousAntiCovid' smartphone app or in paper form as long as the document has a QR code. See the Disneyland Paris website for more details.

Disneyland Paris has increased the frequency of cleaning measures. More than 2000 alcoholic gel distribution points are at your disposal.

Characters no longer greet guests nearby. Instead, they can take photos at a distance. These are known as "selfie spots". Characters do not appear at meals at the moment.

Some entertainment options may be suspended, as well as high-touch areas such as playgrounds, e.g. *La Plage des Pirates*.

Due to the limited capacity of the park, guests must make a reservation to enter in addition to purchasing admission tickets or annual passes. Registration can be done online at www.disneylandparis.com/en-gb/register-tickets/. Customers who purchase tickets for a specific date do not need an additional reservation.

Not all hotels are open. Buffet-style meals are suspended. When the "all you can eat" option is available, you will need to request each dish from a Cast Member. Food offerings are subject to change.

Park Maps and Times Guides are not distributed - you will need to use the official Disneyland Paris app to get this information.

Please check the Disneyland Paris website before visiting to see what sanitary measures are in place during your visit.

Contents

Introduction

Disneyland Paris is Europe's most popular destination, having amassed over 300 million visitors in the last 30 years.

The project for the resort started in the 1980s when Disney executives wanted to bring the magic of Disney theme parks to Europe. This was where the original stories, which inspire many Disney fairy tales, originated.

Disney soon decided to build the resort in France due to its central location and favourable weather when compared to some countries further north in Europe.

The fact that the site was less than a two-hour flight from many European locations sealed the deal. Plus, the French government promised to build infrastructure to access the resort.

Disneyland Park opened in 1992 as a European adaptation of California's Disneyland. Its design was, however, updated to reflect the local culture and to take advantage of all the land the company had purchased.

The project was not without its critics. In 2002, the resort expanded as Walt Disney Studios Park opened as the second park at the resort, providing a portal for movie fanatics.

As well as the two theme parks, guests can enjoy the Disney Village area (free admission), with shopping and dining experiences that cover a range of tastes.

A campsite with an adventure playground and six themed hotels are also on site.

Disneyland Paris is not just a theme park or a place to ride rollercoasters. Guests can meet characters, watch shows and parades, make new friends and enjoy a feeling of magic that no other theme park resort in Europe rivals.

Thrill-seekers may not find the tallest and fastest rides in Europe at the resort, but the quality of the experiences offered is second to none.

2022 is a fantastic time to visit as the resort celebrates its 30th anniversary and opens new attractions and areas.

Disneyland Paris is a place where dreams really do come true for guests every single day, and you are about to become part of it all.

Planning

Planning a trip to Disneyland Paris may seem daunting. You have to think about transport, accommodation, food, park tickets, spending money, and more. This section aims to get you prepared before we delve into more detail.

When to Visit

Crowds at Disneyland Paris vary significantly from season to season and even day to day. The difference in a single day can save you hundreds of euros and hours in queues. You need to consider national and school holidays in France and the surrounding countries, the weather, pricing and more to find the best time to go. Here is our guide of the best times to visit Disneyland Paris, even including a detailed analysis of weekdays.

MAJOR HOLIDAYS (TIMES TO AVOID)

In 2022

- 1st to 3rd January: New Year's Day & School Break
- 4th February to 7th March: French and UK school break, and 30th Anniversary Celebration starts
- 17th March: St. Patrick's Day (celebrations mean slightly bigger crowds)
- 8th April to 9th May: Easter Holidays - Particularly busy from 8th to 26th April.
- 29th April to 2nd May: Labour Day weekend
- 6th to 9th May: Victory in Europe Day weekend
- 25th to 30th May: Ascension Day weekend
- 3rd to 7th June: Pentecost/Whit Sunday
- 12th June to 6th September: European School Summer Break. August is by far the busiest month. July is busier than June. September is less busy from the 7th onwards.
- 14th July: Bastille Day (Bank Holiday)
- 15th August: Assumption Day
- September and October weekends
- 21st October to 7th November: UK and France school holidays, Halloween
- 11th to 14th November - Armistice Day Weekend
- 17th December 2022 to 3rd January 2023 - Christmas Holidays. 31st Dec is the busiest day.

Top Tip: If a public holiday falls on a Friday or a Monday, that weekend becomes a *pont* (a long weekend). If it is on a Thursday or Tuesday, many turn this into a 4-day weekend. Avoid *ponts* as they are always very busy.

Days of the Week

The days of the week that you choose to visit make a large difference in how long you will wait to get on rides. A ride can have a wait time of 90 minutes on one day, and just 30 minutes on the next. The most notable difference is between the busier weekends and the less busy weekdays.

The best day of the week to visit is Tuesday, followed by Thursday, then Wednesday, then Monday, Friday, and Sunday - the busiest day of the week is by far Saturday. Park hours are often extended on weekends to compensate for the larger crowds.

Doing Disney on a Budget

A visit to Disneyland Paris is expensive – it is a premium theme park destination and with travel, park tickets, accommodation, food and souvenirs, it is easy to see why many families save up for a long time for a visit. However, there are many ways to reduce your spending at the resort yet still have a magical time.

1. Drive – Visitors from all across Europe can drive to the resort. Even from the UK, driving is an option - a ferry or Eurotunnel crossing can cost as little as £50-£150 return when booked in advance for a car and all its passengers. From Calais, in France, is it an easy 3-hour drive. There are about €18.50-€22 of tolls each way depending on the route from Calais to Disneyland Paris, plus petrol costs.

2. Budget flights – Flights are available from £30/€40 each way from across Europe to Paris. *Charles de Gaulle* is the most convenient airport, followed by *Orly*. Steer clear of *Paris Beauvais-Tille* Airport, which is 120km away from Disneyland Paris.

3. Take the train – TGV and Eurostar trains can get you to the resort. If travelling across France, try InOui (website: en.oui.sncf), which offers cheap travel on high-speed trains from stations across France.

TGV advance 'Prems' fares are also often good value. You will arrive at *Marne la Vallée – Chessy* station.

For UK guests, Eurostar trains start at £72 return if booked in advance. Those from UK regions can book "through fares" from their home station to Disneyland Paris on Eurostar.com, changing trains at St. Pancras. For example, Manchester to Paris starts at £90 return.

Please note direct Eurostar services from London to Disneyland Paris are currently suspended due to COVID-19, although they should return in 2022.

Trains avoid costly airport transfers.

4. Hotels – Disney hotels are themed but are expensive compared to other nearby hotels, such as the Kyriad, which has offers from €60 per night. However, a non-Disney hotel means no Extra Magic Time and buying park tickets separately.

Alternatively, stay at one of the cheaper Disney hotel such as the Hotel Cheyenne or Hotel Santa Fe to get the on-site benefits.

5. Buy an annual pass – If visiting for at least four days, an annual pass can work out cheaper than a 4-day ticket. Plus, you get dining and merchandise discounts.

6. Use a special offer – There is always a special offer running, whether it is 'kids go free', or an extra day and night free. If there are no offers, wait for one.

7. Tickets – If you are not staying at a Disney hotel, pre-purchase your tickets. Buying them at the ticket booths on the day is more expensive and very time-consuming. They may even be sold out!

8. Eat at Disney Village – *McDonald's, Earl of Sandwich, Vapiano* and *Five Guys* sell fast food at prices cheaper than the food in the theme parks.

9. Meal vouchers – If you are eating at restaurants daily, then pre-purchasing Meal Plans can save you money. They can be added at the time of booking or any time before your trip if staying at a Disney hotel. Vouchers must be purchased for the entire stay.

10. Packed lunches – Make your own packed lunches. There is a huge supermarket called Auchan in the nearby town of *Val d'Europe*. This is a 30-minute walk from the theme parks or a 5-minute bus or taxi journey. Alternatively, bring food and snacks from home.

11. Take your own photos – Skip the official character photo and take one yourself; the Cast Members (Disney employees) will even take the photo for you. If you want official photos, see our section on Disneyland Paris' PhotoPass and PhotoPass+ services for unlimited photos for a set price instead of paying €15 for each one.

12. Take your own merchandise – Buy dresses, outfits and toys from Disney Stores, online or at supermarkets before you visit Disneyland Paris. Give your child the costume or toy once you arrive to avoid the inflated in-park merchandise prices.

13. More affordable meals – Although food prices are high, some restaurants offer better value than others. Try the set menus with a main course, dessert and drink for one price. Or, try a buffet as a late lunch and have a lighter dinner.

Speaking French

All Cast Members at the resort speak French. With very few exceptions, all Cast Members at the resort also speak English.

Therefore, for the most part, the language barrier is not a problem when talking to Cast Members.

However, knowing the basics in French is helpful, and employees do appreciate it if you say *Bonjour* and then switch to English, or even better say *Parlez-vous Anglais?* [pronounced *par-lay-voo-zarn-glay*] for "Do you speak English?".

You may occasionally come across a Cast Member with a limited grasp of the English language, which can make things more difficult but not impossible.

Cast Members often speak many other languages too – Spanish and Italian are very common.

Useful French Phrases

Hello/Good morning – Bonjour [Bon-sjur]
Good evening – Bonsoir [Bon-swar]
Goodbye - Au revoir [Or re-vwar]
Do you speak English? – Parlez-vous anglais? [Par-lay voo-zarn-glay]
How much does this cost? – Combien ça coûte? [Com-byer Sar Coot]
Please – S'il vous plaît [Sill voo-plair]
Thanks – Merci! [Mare-see]
No problem – De rien [De ree-yeah]
A photo of us, please? – Une photo s'il vous plaît? [Oon photo sill voo-plair]
Yes – Oui [We]
No – Non [No – do not pronounce the final 'n']
A little / a bit – Un peu [Um purr]
Rare (for meat) – Saignante [Say-narnte]
Medium-Rare (for meat) – À pointe [Ah pwarnt]
Well-done/well-cooked (for meat) – Bien Cuite [Bee-yen kweet]
Very well-cooked (for meat) – Très Bien Cuite [Treh bee-yen kweet]
One - Un [uh]
Two - Deux [dur]
Three - Trois [Tr-wah]
Four - Quatre [Cat-re]
Five - Cinq [Sunk]

One very useful phrase you will hear when boarding rides is:
Vous êtes combien? - This means "How many in your party?"

Currency and Payment Methods

France uses Euros as its currency. If you come from a country that does not use Euros as its currency, then you can either exchange cash before you go, or use a debit/credit card while in France.

With payment cards, be aware of any fees from your bank for paying in a foreign currency. These are commonly around 2.9% per transaction.

Be sure to warn your bank you will be travelling to avoid your card being blocked for security reasons.

One option for visitors from the UK is to use *CurrenSea* - this is a debit card that reduces fees to just 0.5% or less when abroad. Simply spend on the card and you will be charged to your UK bank account in pounds. The card is free.

Sign up with coupon code "GDSNES" and you'll get £10 free when you spend £100 abroad within four months of signing up. That's free money you can spend on some treats!

Alternatively, a credit or debit card with 0% foreign

exchange fees is even better.
For guests who prefer to exchange money there, you can find Bureau de Changes at both theme parks and in the Disney Village. These operate with limited opening hours and the rates offered are usually poor.

Celebrating Birthdays

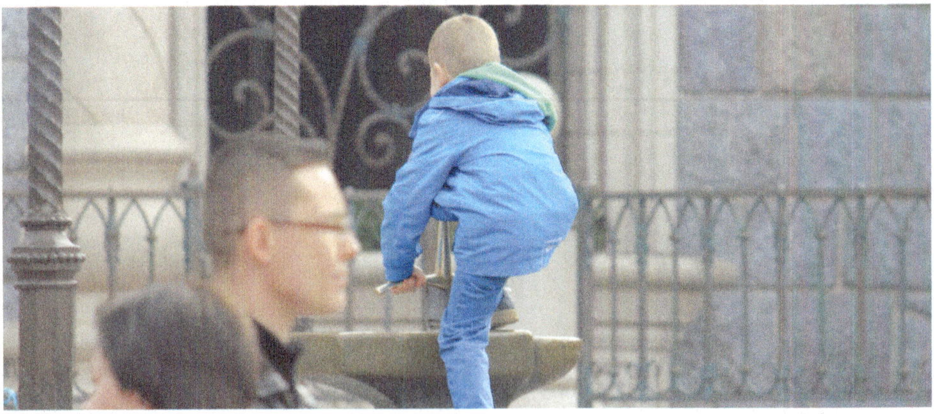

There are several ways to celebrate a birthday at Disneyland Paris. For example, at Table Service restaurants, you can add a birthday cake to your meal for €35.

We recommend making a restaurant reservation by calling the dining booking line and mentioning the cake in advance - you can do this up to 2 months before the big day.

You can also visit Guest Relations (City Hall and Studio Services) to get a 'Happy Birthday' badge to wear during your special day.

To entertain younger guests, make sure to ask the Cast Members at City Hall whether any of the characters have a special birthday message for your child.

You will enter a room where a phone will ring, and when your child picks the phone up, there will be a recorded message wishing them a happy birthday – this can make for some incredible memories.

Getting There

Travelling to Disneyland Paris is simple due to its central location. Options include driving, flying and high-speed trains.

Plane

Flying to Paris is convenient for many visitors as the French capital is under two hours away from most of Europe, and in the era of budget airlines, flying doesn't have to break the bank either. Paris has three airports you fly into:

Charles-de-Gaulle Airport
This is the main Parisian airport and the largest.

o *By High-Speed TGV Train*: From the airport, catch a direct TGV train which takes between 9 and 12 minutes from Terminal 2 to *Marne-La-Vallee – Chessy (Disneyland)* station. You can pre-book online at https://en.oui.sncf/en/. Tickets are €15 to €35 per person each way. The first train is at about 06:45; there are no direct TGV trains after 21:19 (check the schedule online by making a test booking). We recommend buying tickets at the airport instead of pre-booking for a specific train in case of flight delays.

o *By Local RER Train*: From the airport, take the RER B line to *Châtelet-les-Halles* station, then switch to the RER A line to *Marne La Vallée – Chessy*. This costs €17.30 per adult with a travel time of about 1 hour 30 minutes. Children under 10 years of age pay €10.65, and children under 4 travel free.

o *By Coach:* The Magical Shuttle bus goes between the airport and Disneyland Paris and even to many *Val d'Europe*-area hotels. There are up to 22 journeys in each direction daily. Pricing is €23 per adult each way and €10 per child ages 3 to 11. The journey takes about 1 hour each way. Book at magicalshuttle.co.uk. This is not a Disney-run service.
o By Taxi: A taxi costs €90 to €100 each way. This is a well-priced and convenient option for groups.

Orly Airport
Paris' second-largest airport.

o *By Coach*: The Magical Shuttle bus is €23 per adult each way, children pay €10. Coach transfers take about 1 hour each way. Book at magicalshuttle.co.uk. This is not a Disney-run service.

o *By Local RER Train*: Get the Orlyval train (6:00am to 11:00pm) to *Antony Orlyval* station. From *Antony Orlyval*, take the RER B line to *Châtelet-les-Halles* station. There, get the RER A line to *Marne la Vallée – Chessy (Disneyland)* station. The total journey time is 1 hour and 30 minutes. Price: €19.35 per adult and €14.25 per child.

o *By Taxi/Private Van*: Prices are €80 to €135 for parties of 3 to 8 people. This is the cheapest and most comfortable choice for groups.

Paris Beauvais-Tille Airport
This airport is not in Paris and therefore has long transfer times.

o *By Public Transport*: Get a shuttle bus from Beauvais Airport to *Porte Maillot* bus station. This is €16 one-way or €29 return per adult (for children ages 4-11 it is €10 and €20). This bus journey takes 1 hour 15 minutes. At *Porte Maillot*, follow the signs to the Metro and take Line 1 (yellow) to *La Defense* (10 minutes).

At *La Defense,* take the RER A line (red) to *Marne La Vallée – Chessy (Disneyland)* station (50 to 60 minutes – €7.60 per adult, €3.80 per child). The total journey time is about 3 hours and the total cost is about €25 per person.

o *By Shuttle Service*: RSTransports.com provides a shared shuttle or private shuttle from the airport to Disneyland Paris. Prices start at €105 for 4 people. The journey time is about 1 hour 15 minutes.

o *By Taxi*: The taxi fare is about €180 to €200 each way. Alternatively, you can rent a car. The journey is 126km each way.

Train

The Eurostar is the most comfortable option for visitors from the south of the UK, reaching the doorstep of Disneyland Paris in just 2 hours 49 minutes from London, and even more quickly from Ebbsfleet and Ashford. Prices start at £72 (€88) per adult return.

Direct from the UK:
There is one direct train per day that leaves London at 10:14 and arrives at 14:03 at *Marne la Vallée-Chessy* Station (Disneyland). Please note this direct service is temporarily suspended due to COVID-19.

Return direct trains depart Disneyland Paris at either 16:55 or 18:01 depending on the day of the week. There are no direct trains on Tuesdays, Thursdays and Saturdays, except during British school holidays.

This service is convenient with security, immigration and check-in usually done in around 15 minutes.

Indirect via Lille:
As there is only one direct Eurostar service per day (and none on some days), you may want to use the indirect option, giving you more flexibility. It is also often cheaper than the direct train.

Passengers board a Eurostar train in the UK (usually with the destination of Brussels) and disembark at *Lille Europe* station - about 1 hour and 20 minutes from London. At *Lille Europe,* passengers wait around 30 minutes for their connecting TGV train from *Lille Europe* to *Marne la Vallée - Chessy* Station (Disneyland).

The whole journey takes as little as 2h53m from London with a 28-minute stopover. Some stopovers are longer, however, so your journey may take up to 4 hours 8 minutes.

The Eurostar website does not usually show indirect trains more than 12 weeks in advance.

Changing trains is easy - you look for the number of your next train on the departure board and go to that platform. Thirty minutes is plenty of time to change, as there are no security or immigration checks here. When on the platform itself, check that you are on the correct train, as there may be multiple trains on the same platform.

On a multi-train booking, if one of your trains is delayed, you will be put on the next one at no extra charge.

The TGV train from *Lille - Europe* makes several stops. It only stops at *Marne-La-Vallee - Chessy* (Disneyland) for a few minutes - make sure not to miss your stop; it is not the end of the route.

There is a helpful video of this process available from 'Disneyland Paris Advice' called "Eurostar indirect via Lille" on Youtube at http://bit.ly/dlplillechange.

Top Tip

Do not book your Eurostar travel with Disneyland Paris as part of a package without checking prices direct with Eurostar. It often works out significantly more expensive to book transportation with Disneyland Paris. We usually recommend booking your train directly at www.eurostar.com. The exception is when Disney has an offer such as free travel for children when it can be cheaper to book with Disneyland Paris. As such, we recommend you check both options. You can book Eurostar trains between 3 and 6 months in advance, depending on the season and route.

International Train + RER (via central Paris): Disneyland Paris is about 32km from central Paris, and the city centre is connected to the theme parks by the fast and frequent RER train service.

Therefore, you can get a high-speed international train to Paris city centre, followed by a local RER train to Disneyland Paris.

This offers you a lot of flexibility – for example, there are up to 18 Eurostar departures per day from London to Paris.

If arriving at *Paris – Gare du Nord* station by Eurostar, it takes a further 50 to 60 minutes to reach Disneyland Paris.

At the time of writing, a ticket on the Paris RER train from Gare du Nord to *Marne-La-Vallée* (Disneyland Paris) costs €7.60 per adult and €3.80 for a child under 10 years old. Follow the signs at *Gare du Nord* for 'Metro & RER' trains.

Take the RER B line in the direction of *Robinson*, *Antony* or *Saint Rémy-lès-Chevreuse* for one stop to *Châtelet-Les Halles*. Here you transfer to RER A line by walking to the adjacent platform and getting a train in the direction of *Marne La Vallée – Chessy.*

Use the information screens to check that the train is going to *Marne La Vallée – Chessy* station (your destination).

Marne La Vallée - Chessy (Disneyland) is the last stop on the RER A line. This journey takes about 40 minutes.

Disney Express

If you have booked your train as part of a package with Disney, you will have the Disney Express luggage transfer service included. This allows you to drop off your bags at the train station on arrival and head straight to the parks.

At *Marne-La-Vallée* Station, follow the signs to the Disney Express counters on the top floor (open 8:00 am to 9:30 pm daily).

Here, you check-in for your hotel and receive your Magic Card (digital park tickets, room key and Meal Plans). Leave your bags with the Cast Members at the desk and they will be taken to the luggage storage area in your hotel. Now, enjoy the theme parks!

This service is available on both direct and indirect Eurostar services, as well as for guests arriving via TGV at *Marne La Vallée - Chessy* station.

If you booked your train separately, this service is available for €15 per person each way.

Driving

You have two options to reach Disneyland Paris if driving from the UK.

The Eurotunnel is a train service that allows passengers and vehicles to travel together from Folkestone (England) and arrive in Calais (France) in 35 minutes.

Alternatively, you can take your car on the ferry from Dover (England) to Calais (France). P&O Ferries is a popular company. The ferry crossing is often cheaper than the Eurotunnel but takes about 90 minutes.

From Calais, it is a 3 hour 30-minute drive to Disneyland Paris. This 290km (180 mi) journey will cost about €18.50 to €22 in tolls and €35 to €45 in fuel each way.

Disneyland Paris has a huge car park for both theme parks. The price of parking for a day is € 30 for cars, € 25 for motorcycles and € 45 for motorhomes. Premium parking spots are € 45 per day. You will have free parking at your hotel and the entrance to the Disney theme parks if you are staying at one of the Disney hotels or the Algonquin's Explorers Hotel.

For those staying in other partner hotels, the cost is 30 € per day (however, if you book your stay through Disneyland Paris, parking is free). The parking lot typically opens at 8:00 a.m. and closes 30 minutes after the closure of both parks.

Hotels

Disneyland Paris owns and operates seven on-site resort hotels, each themed to a different part of America – one is even a campsite where you can stay in log cabins. When booking a hotel directly with Disneyland Paris, your hotel price also includes your park entry tickets.

Advantages of staying at a Disneyland Paris hotel:
- A front desk staffed 24 hours a day
- Friendly Cast Members with knowledge of the resort
- Make dining reservations in person without needing to leave your hotel
- The option to pre-pay for all your meals at the hotel and the theme parks.
- Detailed theming and total immersion
- A stay in the heart of the Disney magic
- Extra Magic Time is available daily. EMT allows hotel guests entry into one or both parks one hour before other guests. During EMT attraction wait times are very short or non-existent.
- Walking distance to the theme parks: 20 minutes or less.
- Free shuttle service from all the hotels to the theme parks (except Disney's Davy Crockett Ranch)
- Meet Disney characters at the hotel during your stay.
- Disney Shopping Service: If you buy merchandise in the parks before 3:00pm, you can have it delivered to your hotel to be collected in the evening, leaving your hands free.
- Park admission tickets are included in all reservations unless otherwise stated.

Dining Key:
€ (Under €15)
€€ (€16 to €29)
€€€ (€30 to €39)
€€€€ (€40 to €49)
€€€€€ (€50+)

Prices relate to set menus for one person where available.

PLMP = Some options on the menu are available on the Plus Meal Plan
STMP = Some options on the menu are available on the Standard Meal Plan
BRMP = Some options on the menu are available on the Breakfast Meal Plan

Learn more about meal plans on page 41.

CHUCK

Pricing:
When booking your hotel, your arrival date determines the price for your entire stay (e.g. if you arrive on a date within the Value pricing season and the remaining days of your holiday are in the Moderate pricing season, your whole stay is charged at the Value price).

This can also work either for or against you as your arrival date could be in the High Season and your other nights in the Regular Season. In this case, you will pay the High Season rate for the entire duration.

There are two solutions: change your dates, or book one package for the more expensive night(s) and then another separate package for the cheaper remaining night(s). You may have to leave your room and re-check in if you do this. If you book two back-to-back stays, ask the Cast Member checking you in whether you can keep the same room.

To see what season you will arrive in, use the live booking function on disneylandparis.com.

A booking agent may be able to advise what the best option for you is if you book over the phone.

More on Pricing

Room prices in this section are based on arrivals until 31st March 2023.

Prices listed are per night and include park tickets for all days of your stay, including check-in and check-out days.

Prices are per room per night for a standard room based on two adults sharing. Additional adults after the second pay a nightly surcharge.

Children under 3 always stay free; children 3 to 11 pay a child price, but there are often sales where the fee is waived for kids.

Multiple-night stays carry a lower "per night" cost. The per-night cost after the third night is 45% to 85% cheaper, as most visitors will not need more than four days to visit the resort. This can make an extended stay at the hotels much better value for money overall.

Magic Card:
The Magic Card is exclusive to the seven Disneyland Paris operated hotels and is given to you at check-in.

It allows you to enter the theme parks including during Extra Magic Time, access to the hotel pools, and free parking both at the hotel and the theme park parking lot, as well as acting as your room key and storing meal plan credits.

During check-in, you can also link a credit or debit card to your Magic Card, which will allow you to pay for food and merchandise at most resort locations using the Magic Card instead of paying with your credit card or in cash each time. You then settle the bill when checking out and pay one lump sum.

This can be a good option for guests from non-euro countries whose credit banks charge a per-transaction foreign currency fee. Just be sure to monitor your spending to not go over budget.

Note: Some small stalls (such as those selling drinks or popcorn) do not accept the Magic Card or credit/debit cards, and only take cash. Disney does not operate most restaurants in Disney Village, so most of these do not accept the Magic Card – but do ask.

How to book your stay:
We recommend booking Disneyland Paris hotels or packages through the official website at www.disneylandparis.com.

The website offers you several room types, but suites must be booked over the phone. Both the Disneyland Paris website and phone reservations charge a £25 booking fee (booking fees are suspended during COVID-19).

Disneyland Paris regularly runs promotions with savings of 10-50% off the regular price, or 'get free nights' deals when you book a stay. If there is not a sale when you are thinking of booking, we recommend waiting as sales run throughout the entire year.

Offers vary seasonally and between different countries. These can be anything from 'free hotel, park tickets and transport for under 12s' to 'free half board meal plans', or even 40% or 50% off a stay. A minimum stay of two or three nights usually applies to promotions, as well as date restrictions.

Booking Tips

Tip 1: You can book Disneyland Paris (and partner) hotels over the phone. Phone booking allows you to pay in instalments instead of one lump sum, with no interest. This allows you to modify your reservation up until you have paid the full amount. So, if a better offer becomes available after you book, you can make changes until the final balance is paid, such as upgrading your hotel or adding meal vouchers. (During COVID-19, booking via the website also allows increased flexibility)

Tip 2: Disneyland Paris runs different promotions in different areas of Europe simultaneously. The good news is you can book any of the promotions from any country. Visit www.disneylandparis.com - at the top of the page select another country, and then try booking through there. You will pay in the currency local to that country. The website's language may also change when you do this. You can also do this by calling Disneyland Paris directly and stating the specific offer you would like to book.

Here is an example of the different promotions available at the time of writing this guide. The UK Disneyland Paris website offered 30% off stays. Whereas, the Spanish website offered 25% off stays, a €200 gift card and kids go free under age 7. Clearly, these are very different offers with different savings depending on your needs.

Disneyland Hotel

This 565-room, 27-suite, Art Deco/Victorian Hotel is the height of luxury at Disneyland Paris. It is located at the entrance of Disneyland Park and is only 3 minutes away from Walt Disney Studios Park.

CLOSED

This hotel is currently being refurbished and is closed with no reopening date announced at the time of writing. Check disneylandparis.com for further updates.

The Disneyland Hotel is the most expensive and luxurious place to stay at Disneyland Paris.
Some rooms have views over Disneyland Park, or over Fantasia Gardens in front of the hotel.

The hotel has many dining options. At California Grill, you can even enjoy the fireworks from the balcony during your dinner.

The Celestia Spa offers facials from €95 and body treatments from €55. Massages start at €60 for 20 minutes and kids spa experiences start at €60.

Castle Club rooms are "club level" and offer a lounge area with complimentary non-alcoholic beverages during the day, and a perfect view of the fireworks through the windows at night. At Castle Club, characters appear in the morning and sometimes in the evening. There is even a private lift directly to the turnstiles without walking through the rest of the hotel. This is a truly unique, premium experience.

A 'Princess or Pirate for a Day' experience is available, including for non-hotel guests. Here children get a makeover with costumes, accessories and more. Pricing starts at €120.

Room Size: 34m^2 for standard rooms (up to 4 people, plus one child under 3 years old in a cot), and 58m^2 in the Castle Club Suites. Other suites go up to 187m^2 – including the Sleeping Beauty suite, the Cinderella suite, Tinker Bell suite and Walt's Apartment suite. Family rooms (up to 5 people with one on a sofa bed), and Castle Club rooms (up to 4 people – phone bookings only) are also available.

Breakfast: Extra charge. €36 per adult and €27 per child.

Standard Room Prices (before refurbishment):
1 night: €894 to €1468
2 nights: €1538 to €2686
3 nights: €2174 to €3896.
Castle Club rooms are an additional €470+ per night.

Activities: An indoor pool, sauna, steam bath and fitness suite are complimentary. There is a "Club Minnie" Playroom, children's corner, and an arcade. Dry cleaning is available at a surcharge.

Extras: Free Wi-Fi is available, including in guests' rooms.

Dining

Inventions (€€€€€) – Buffet Service. Lunch with Disney characters from 12:30pm to 3:00pm. Dinner with Disney characters from 6:00pm to 10:30pm. Plus, a themed brunch with the Disney Characters is served from 1:00pm to 3:00pm on Sundays.
California Grill (€€€€€) – Table Service. Set menus vary from €70 to €130 for adults; €38 for children. Disney states, "Shoulders must be covered for men. Bermuda shorts, shorts and flip flops are not permitted." Open for dinner only.
Café Fantasia – Hotel Bar, serving drinks and snacks. Serves cocktails, champagne, other wines, soft drinks and hot drinks.

Disney's Hotel New York - The Art of Marvel

This Art Deco, New York-themed hotel features 565 rooms and 27 suites, and is a mere 10-minute walk to the parks. A shuttle bus is also available.

Themed to an apartment block in the Big Apple, this is the second closest hotel to the parks, and is located by the entrance of Disney Village and Lake Disney.

In June 2021, the hotel reopened following an extensive refurbished with a Marvel theme throughout, including over 350 pieces of art by over 110 artists from around the world.

Room Size: 31m² in standard rooms (for 4 people). Empire State Club lodging includes Club Rooms and Club Suites (ranging from 56m² to 166m²).

Breakfast: Extra charge. €28 per day per adult and €23 per child.

Standard Room Prices:
1 night: €449 to €1172
2 nights: €729 to €2094
3 nights: €1269 to €3012
4 nights: €1662 to €3972.

Activities: Complimentary heated outdoor and indoor pools, adults-only steam rooms, tennis courts and a gym. Massages are available for a fee. Hotel guests only can access Marvel Superhero Photo Spots and meet Spider-Man, as well as enjoy the Marvel Design Studio kids area.

Extras: Free Wi-Fi access throughout the hotel, including rooms. Dry cleaning is available. Suites and Empire State Club rooms are also available in addition to standard rooms - breakfast is included in these rooms.

Dining

Manhattan Restaurant (€€€€) [PLMP] – Offers an Italian menu, under the "Chandelier of Asgard". Dinner only.
Downtown Restaurant (€€€€) [PLMP, BRMP] – Serves Chinese, American and Italian cuisine. Also serves breakfast.
Skyline Bar – Enjoy simulated "top of a skyscraper" views as Iron Man zips by.
Bleecker St. Lounge – A hip loft-style hangout.

Disney's Newport Bay Club

This New-England style hotel features 1093 rooms and 13 suites. It is a 15-minute walk to the parks, or a free shuttle bus journey away.

Themed to New England, this nautical-inspired hotel houses two restaurants and anchors one end of Lake Disney. It is the fourth closest hotel to the parks.

It is one of our favourite hotels in terms of design but it can often feel a bit overwhelming with its huge size.

Room Size: Standard rooms are 27m^2; family rooms for up to 6 guests are also available. Suites include the Admiral's Floor at 27m^2, Honeymoon Suites from 50m^2 to 63m^2, The Resort Suite at 55m^2 and the Presidential Suite measuring 84m^2.

Breakfast: Extra charge. €28 per day per adult and €23 per child.

Guests saying in Compass Club Rooms have access to a complimentary breakfast.

Standard Room Prices:
1 night: €341 to €958
2 nights: €527 to €1666
3 nights: €962 to €2370
4 nights: €1256 to €3116.

For Compass Club rooms, add an extra €176 per room per night.

Activities: Indoor and outdoor pool, with deckchairs; sauna/steam bath and a gym. There is an indoor kids play area.

Extras: Free Wi-Fi access throughout the hotel and in guest rooms. This hotel has a convention centre. Dry cleaning is available at a surcharge.

Dining

Yacht Club (€€€€€) [PLMP] – Table Service. Serves New England specialities with Mediterranean influences.
Cape Cod (€€€) [PLMP, BRMP] – Buffet. Also serves breakfast as well as lunch and dinner.
Captain's Quarters – Hotel Bar, serving drinks and snacks.

Disney's Sequoia Lodge

Recreating the ambience of the American National Parks, the Sequoia Lodge's 1011 rooms and 14 suites are a 15-minute walk from the parks. A shuttle is also available.

Disney's Sequoia Lodge is our favourite on-site hotel as far as value for money is concerned.

It is a mid-priced hotel, but it is slightly closer to the parks than the pricier *Newport Bay Club Hotel*.

We feel this hotel is one of the best themed on property with a fantastic lounge and pool.

Note: *Disney's Sequoia Lodge*'s facade is undergoing an enhancement project that will continue until Autumn 2022. The swimming pool and fitness centre will be closed from mid-January to Summer 2022. Other activities and services at the hotel will not be affected.

Room Size: 22m^2 in a standard room. Golden Forest Club rooms (with a private lounge with snacks) are also available, as are Honeymoon Suites and Hospitality Suites (55m^2).

Breakfast: Extra charge. €24 per day per adult and €17 per child. Breakfast is included in Golden Forest Club rooms.

Standard Room Prices:
1 night: €277 to €844
2 nights: €413 to €1438
3 nights: €767 to €2028
4 nights: €997 to €2660.

Golden Forest Club rooms are an extra €80 per person per night.

Activities: Indoor and outdoor pool, a gym, and sauna/steam bath. Massages are available for an extra charge. Kids play areas are also available.

Extras: Free Wi-Fi access throughout the hotel, including in rooms.

Dining

Hunter's Grill and Beaver Creek Tavern (€€€) [BRMP, PLMP] – Buffet in a rustic lodge-like setting.
Redwood Bar and Lounge – This amazing Hotel Bar and Lounge is undoubtedly one of our favourites. You can't help but feel you are in the middle of the American wilderness with the huge fireplace and cosy chairs. This is the perfect stop during winter evenings.

Disney's Hotel Cheyenne

Themed to America's Old Wild West, with details from the Toy Story films, this 1000 room hotel is a 20-minute walk from the parks. A shuttle is also available.

Disney's Hotel Cheyenne, along with *Disney's Hotel Santa Fe*, are the resort's budget hotels and are the most affordable ways to stay at an official Disneyland Paris hotel.

The rooms and services on offer are more basic than the other hotels. For example, you won't have access to a pool or gym, but you still have access to Extra Magic Time (early theme park entry), and you can walk to the theme parks (or get a complimentary shuttle).

In terms of overall theming, we feel that this is one of the most well-themed hotels with the buildings shaped to look like they are part of the Wild West.

Room Size: Standard rooms measure 21m^2.

Breakfast: Extra charge. €21 per day per adult and €14 per child.

Standard Room Prices:
1 night: €264 to €786
2 nights: €418 to €1322
3 nights: €505 to €1854
4 nights: €648 to €2428.

Activities: Video games room; outdoor and indoor kids play areas; seasonal pony rides are available for an extra charge.

Extras: Free Wi-Fi is available in the bar, lobby and guest rooms.

Dining

Chuck Wagon Café (€€€) [PLMP, BRMP] – Buffet. A continental breakfas is available. Dinner is a buffet.
Red Garter Saloon – Hotel Bar, serving snacks and drinks.
Starbucks (€) – Snacks, sandwiches and coffees from the world-famous chain.

Disney's Hotel Santa Fe

Themed to Santa Fe, in South West America, and with nods to Pixar's 'Cars' films. This 1000 room hotel is a 20-minute walk from the parks. A shuttle is also available.

Disney's Hotel Cheyenne, along with *Disney's Hotel Santa Fe*, are the resort's budget hotels and are the most affordable ways to stay at an official Disneyland Paris hotel.

The rooms and services on offer are more basic than the other hotels. For example, you won't have access to a pool or gym, but you still have access to Extra Magic Time (early theme park entry), and you can walk to the theme parks (or get a complimentary shuttle).

In terms of theming, this is our least favourite hotel - the buildings do resemble some in real Santa Fe, but it is not the most magical of themes. This hotel is usually slightly cheaper than *Disney's Hotel Cheyenne*.

This hotel is also marginally further away from the theme parks than *Disney's Hotel Cheyenne*, making it the furthest from the parks. Despite that, it is still much more convenient than any non-official hotel, and the rooms have fun Cars-themed touches.

Room Size: A standard room measures 21m^2 (sleeps up to 4 people plus 1 child under 3 years in a cot). Family rooms for up to 6 people are also available.

Breakfast: Extra charge. €21 per day per adult and €14 per child.

Standard Room Prices:
1 night: €254 to €735
2 nights: €367 to €1219
3 nights: €476 to €1699
4 nights: €610 to €2222.

Activities: A video game arcade is available.

Extras: Free Wi-Fi is available throughout the hotel, including in rooms.

Dining

La Cantina (€€€) [STMP, BRMP] – Dinner buffet from 6:00pm to 10:30pm. A continental breakfast is also available.
Rio Grande Bar – Hotel Bar.
Starbucks Coffee (€) – Snacks, sandwiches and coffees from the world-famous chain.

Disney's Davy Crockett Ranch

Unlike the other Disney accommodation, Davy Crockett Ranch is not a hotel, but a 595-cabin campsite.

CLOSURE

This campsite is closed until 31st March 2022.

At *Disney's Davy Crockett Ranch*, you do not stay in a hotel room, but a large log cabin instead. Each cabin is private to you and your party only.

You truly do feel a world away from the theme parks in a serene environment. This accommodation is ideal for large groups with rooms for up to 6 people.

Davy Crockett Ranch is not located near any of the other on-site hotels. It is also further than most of the partner hotels as it is an 8km (15-minute) drive to the theme parks - you must provide your own transport as shuttle buses are not available.

Room Size: There are both 1-bedroom (36m^2) and 2-bedroom (39m^2) cabins available. Cabins sleep up to 6 people. A Premium 2-bedroom cabin option is also available.

Breakfast: Extra charge - €12 per person (all ages).

Standard Cabin Prices:
1 night: €299 to €628
2 nights: €457 to €894
3 nights: €612 to €1321
4 nights: €791 to €1739.

Activities: There is a beautiful heated indoor swimming pool at this resort, as well as tennis courts, a video games arcade, pony rides, quad bikes, indoor and outdoor children's play areas, a small farm and an adventure ropes course *(Davy's Crockett Adventure)*. Some activities require a surcharge.

Extras: Free Wi-Fi is available at the restaurant and the bar. In-room wired internet access is available at a surcharge. Daily cleaning of cabins is an extra charge. The Alamo Trading Post shop sells food, clothes and souvenirs.

Dining

Davy Crockett's Tavern (€€€) [PLMP] – Buffet in a woodland tavern.
Crockett's Saloon – Hotel Bar.

Les Villages Nature Paris

Les Villages Nature was created in partnership between Pierre et Vacances and Disney. Think of it as a French version of the British Centerparcs.

This unique experience is not an official Disneyland Paris hotel - nor is this actually at Disneyland Paris. However, it is a popular place to stay and Disney sells room-and-ticket packages where you stay at *Les Villages Nature*.

Les Villages Natures is designed to be an example of sustainable living with guests staying in apartments surrounded by nature. The resort is built around a huge indoor waterpark called the *Aqualagon* where the water is heated by geothermal energy.

Les Villages Nature is around a 15-minute drive from Disneyland Paris, or 25 minutes by using the public bus route (a small charge applies).

This accommodation is perfect for large groups with apartments for up to 6 people.

Room Size: There are 1-bedroom (44 m^2), 2-bedroom (52 m^2) and 3-bedroom (65 m^2) apartments available. These sleep up to 6 people. Premium cabins are also available.

Breakfast: Extra charge.

Standard 1-Bedroom Prices:
1 night: €293 to €812
2 nights: €391 to €1280
3 nights: €488 to €1748
4 nights: €586 to €2216.

Activities: Indoor waterpark and geothermal outdoor lagoon, "extraordinary gardens" to explore, pony club, indoor play area, outdoor play area, lake beach (swimming in summer only), aerial obstacle trails (extra charge), fitness trail, spa, bowling alley, and bike rentals.

Extras: Free Wi-Fi is available. A bakery, mini-market, farmers market. bars and restaurants are available on site. Laundry facilities are available.

Dining

Aqualagon Café – Refreshments, snacks and treats.
Bowling Alley Bar – Hotel Bar.
Lakeside Promenade – Many options from counter service to quick service, bistro to a wine bar, and healthy meals to gourmet delicacies.

Partner Hotels

Partner hotels are located just outside the main Disneyland Paris area. These are often much more affordable than Disney's hotels. Sample room prices are supplied by Disneyland Paris and include theme park tickets. You can also book these hotels independently without park tickets.

Radisson Blu Hotel

Number of Rooms: 250 guest rooms and suites.
Room Size: Standard room (30m^2, maximum occupancy: 2 adults and 1 child aged under 3), Family room (30m^2, maximum occupancy: up to 4 adults), Junior Suite (60m^2), Suite (70m^2) and Presidential Suite (90m^2).
Breakfast: Included in most rates.
Room Prices: Sample price per person per night (based on 2 adults per room): €279.50
Activities: Swimming pool, fitness centre, spa, and outdoor play area. Next to a golf course, with 9 and 18-hole courses available to play on (extra charge).
Extras: Free Wi-Fi throughout the hotel including in rooms. Meeting rooms available.
Dining: Pamplemousse – French Table Service; Birdie – Buffet; and Le Chardon – Bar.

Dream Castle Hotel

Number of Rooms: 397 rooms and suites.
Room Size: Double rooms and family rooms (28m^2), double queen rooms (44m^2), Rapunzel suite (54m^2), The Baron von Münchhausen Suite (60m^2) and The Royal Suite (220m^2).
Breakfast: Included in most rates.
Room Prices: Sample price per person per night (based on 2 adults per room): €235.50
Activities: Swimming pool, fitness centre, spa, indoor and outdoor play area, carousel, and a video game room.
Extras: Free Wi-Fi is available throughout the hotel including in guest rooms.
Dining: The Market Restaurant – Buffet/Table Service; and Excalibur – Bar.

Magic Circus Hotel

Number of Rooms: 396 rooms and suites.
Room Size: Double rooms and family rooms (28m^2), and suites (up to 60m^2).
Breakfast: Included in most rates.
Room Prices: Sample price per person per night (based on 2 adults per room): €232
Activities: Swimming pool and fitness centre.
Extras: Free Wi-Fi is available throughout the hotel including in guest rooms.
Dining: L'Etoile – Buffet; and Bar des Artistes – Bar

Adagio ApartHotel Marne la Valle - Val d'Europe

Number of Rooms: 290 rooms and suites.
Room Size: Studios (21m^2), 1 to 3 bedroom apartments (27m^2 to 53m^2)
Breakfast: Included in most rates.
Room Prices: Sample price per person per night (based on 2 adults per room): €218
Activities: Swimming pool.
Extras: Free Wi-Fi throughout the hotel, including in rooms.
Dining: There is no restaurant (except the buffet breakfast room). Guest rooms include kitchenettes to cook meals.

Explorers Hotel

Number of Rooms: 390 rooms.
Room Size: Standard crew rooms measure 18m^2 to 22m^2.
Breakfast: Included in most rates.
Room Prices: Sample price per person per night (based on 2 adults per room): €247
Activities: Swimming pool, play areas, video games room, and kids fitness area.
Extras: Free Wi-Fi is available throughout the hotel including in guest rooms. Themed suites are also available including Planet Hollywood, Sweet and Jungle themes.
Dining: La Plantation – Buffet; Captain's Library – Table Service; Marco's Pizza – Quick Service; and Smuggler's Tavern and Trader's Cafe Bar – Bar

Hotel l'Elysée - Val d'Europe

Number of Rooms: 152 rooms, including 4 executive suites.
Room Size: Cosy rooms (24m^2 - 2 person limit), family rooms (24m^2 - 4 person limit), family XL rooms (up to 48m^2 - 8 person limit) and exec suites (38m^2 - 4 person limit).
Breakfast: Included in most rates.
Room Prices: Sample price per person per night (based on 2 adults per room): €220
Activities: None.
Extras: Free Wi-Fi is available throughout the hotel including in guest rooms. Meeting rooms are available. Laundry is available for an additional charge. 1-minute walk to *Val d'Europe* RER train station.
Dining: Le George – Table Service (lunch only); and Le Diplomate – Bar.

Campanile Val de France

Number of Rooms: 300 rooms.
Room Size: Standard rooms measure 18.5m^2 for up to 4 people.
Breakfast: Included in most rates.
Room Prices: Sample price per person per night (based on 2 adults per room): €212
Activities: Carousel, video games room, and indoor children's play area.
Extras: Free Wi-Fi is available throughout the hotel including in guest rooms.
Dining: Le Marché Gourmand – Buffet; and L'Abreuvoir – Bar.

B&B Hotel

Number of Rooms: 400 rooms.
Room Size: Standard rooms measure 15m^2 for up to 5 people.
Breakfast: Included in most rates.
Room Prices: Sample price per person per night (based on 2 adults per room): €209.50
Activities: Carousel and video games room.
Extras: Free Wi-Fi is available throughout the hotel, including in guest rooms.
Dining: Breakfast – Buffet; Les Halles - Snack Bar; and BAR - Bar.

More about Partner Hotels

Partner Hotels have no Disney theming, but they are kid-friendly and the staff have *some* knowledge of the theme parks. All these hotels provide frequent shuttle buses, and the longest shuttle bus ride is only 10 minutes. Wait times for buses may be up to 25 minutes in the low season; buses run every 10 to 15 minutes at peak times.

Most of the hotels also have a Disney shop where in-park purchases can be delivered. Partner hotels do not generally include city taxes when booked – these must be paid at check-in and are about €1-€2 per adult per night. If you don't wish to book a package with tickets, use a hotel aggregator such as Hotels.com. For packages, book directly at Disneyland Paris.com

Tickets

There are many ways to buy park entry tickets for Disneyland Paris. Prices, special offers, and ticket lengths vary depending on where and when you buy your tickets. To help you choose the best option for you, here is a detailed look at Disneyland Paris' ticket options.

Important: If you have booked a Disney hotel through the Disneyland Paris website or over the phone, you can skip this section as park tickets are included in your package unless you specifically make a room-only reservation.

At the Park

Guests who turn up at Disneyland Paris spontaneously can buy tickets at the booths at the entrance of each theme park. As at the park you are a captive market, 'gate prices' (purchased on-site at Disneyland Paris) are the most expensive. You can get a substantial discount by booking in advance. Plus, you'll save *a lot* of time.

You can purchase one-park or two-park tickets for one or multiple days at any of the ticket booths. As well as the staffed ticket booths, there are also automated ticket booths under the Disneyland Hotel.

Please note on-site ticket sales are suspended during Covid-19.

Disney Stores

You can buy tickets at any Disney Store in the UK for Disneyland Paris and most Disney Stores around Europe. Tickets for Disneyland Paris may also be stocked at selected other Disney Stores worldwide. Just ask at the counter.

These tickets are priced the same as at the theme park ticket booths, but will save you time at the resort as you can head directly to the turnstiles instead of queuing to buy tickets. If you are buying in advance, then we recommend you do so online to get the largest savings.

Gate Ticket Prices

1 day/1 park
Adults: €99;
Children: €91

1 day/2 parks
Adults: €119;
Children: €111

2 days/2 parks
Adult: €179;
Child: €165

3 days/2 parks
Adult: €219;
Child: €201

4 days/2 parks
Adult: €259;
Child: €238

Children are classed as 3 to 11 year olds. Children under 3 enter for free – proof of age may be requested.

The ticket booths for Disneyland Park are located under the pink Disneyland Hotel. Ticket booths for the Walt Disney Studios Park are located to the right of the park's entrance turnstiles.

Online

If you purchase your tickets in advance online, you can make significant savings on the standard prices. The price varies depending on the date of your visit and the visit length.

1-Day Tickets:
- Lowest Season – Adult: €54; Child: €50
- Low Season – Adult: €59; Child: €54
- Medium Season – Adult: €79; Child: €73
- High Season – Adult: €89; Child: €82
- Peak Season – Adult: €94; Child: €86

Discounted single-day tickets bought online can be purchased up to one day before the date of your visit. They cannot be used on the day of purchase itself unless you buy a full-priced ticket online. You must choose the date of your visit in advance to enjoy the lower rates.

If you opt to have the tickets posted to your home address (additional charges apply), the tickets must be purchased at least 10 days before the date of your visit. Or, you can simply print them off straight away.

2-Park tickets allow you to visit both parks on the same day.

Multi-Day Tickets:

• 2 days/2 parks
Adult: €179; Child: €165

• 3 days/2 parks
Adult: €219; Child: €201

• 4 days/2 parks
Adult: €259; Child: €238

At the time of writing, in January 2022, it was not possible to buy multi-day tickets online. You had to buy each day individually.

Ticket Brokers

There are online ticket brokers that provide genuine attraction tickets, sometimes with big savings! We recommend Attraction Tickets Direct, and AttractionTix.

Due to Covid-19, to control the number of visitors inside the park at any time you must register undated tickets in advance before entering the park. If your tickets were included in a hotel package booked with Disneyland Paris, this has been done for you. If you purchase a ticket with a specific date, this is already done.

If you have purchased an undated ticket, you must register to enter the theme parks at www.disneylandparis.com/en-gb/register-tickets/.

Annual Passes

A Disneyland Paris Annual Pass gives you a year of benefits for the price of a few days' entry. Passes are available to all visitors. While Disneyland Paris is operating the reservation system for tickets, you must book the dates of your visit in advance online.

Discovery: €209	**Magic Flex: €299**	**Magic Plus: €329**	**Infinity: €479**
Access to the parks 150 days per year. Cannot be used on the 2nd and 3rd day after activation.	Access to the parks 300 days per year.	Access to the parks 350 days per year.	Access to the parks 365 days per year.
Unlimited parking add-on for €60.	Unlimited parking is included.	Unlimited parking is included.	Unlimited parking is included.
	Shops: 10% discount	Shops: 10% discount	Shops: 20% discount
	Dining: 10% discount	Dining: 10% discount	Dining: 15% discount
	Discounts on Disney hotel rooms.	Discounts on Disney hotel rooms.	Discounts on Disney hotel rooms.
	20% off 1-day park entry tickets for family/friends	20% off 1-day park entry tickets for family/friends	20% off 1-day park entry tickets for family/friends
	1-Year PhotoPass add-on for €65	1-Year PhotoPass add-on for €59	1-Year PhotoPass included
		10% off at French Disney Stores	10% off at French Disney Stores
		Ten 1 day/2 park tickets each year for €42 each in low season and €57 in high season.	Twenty 1 day/2 park tickets each year for €37 each in low season and €52 in high season.
		Dedicated park entrances, and access to Extra Magic Time	Dedicated park entrances, access to Extra Magic Time, free locker, pushchair, kennel and wheelchair rentals.

Pricing and annual pass benefits are valid until 30th March 2022 and may change after this date. We are expecting a radical overhaul of the passes to take place in the next year or so. Annual passholders must also register their visits as if they were regular undated park tickets (see the previous page for more information).

Should I get an annual pass?

If you are visiting for three days or longer, consider getting an annual pass as it gives you discounts on food, hotels, merchandise and more. One pass can get you discounts for the entire group. An annual pass also makes sense if you are planning to return within a year.

An annual pass even makes sense on shorter trips if you are a big foodie or love shopping for merchandise.

Annual Pass Blockout Dates

Discovery Pass:
December 2021: Every Sat and Sun, plus 20 to 31
January 2022: 1, 2, 8, 9, 15, 22 and 29
February 2022: 5 to 28
March 2022: 1-6, 12, 13, 19, 20 and 26

In addition to the above dates, the Discovery Pass can NOT be used the two days following purchase.

Magic Flex Pass:
October 2021: 18 to 31
November 2021: None
December 2021: 18 to 31
January 2022: Every Wednesday and Thursday
February 2022: None
March 2022: None

Magic Plus Pass:
October 2021: 30 and 31
November 2021: None
December 2021: 25 to 31
January 2022: None
February 2022: None
March 2022: None

Unfortunately Disneyland Paris has not released blockout dates for passes for after 30th March 2022.

Blackout dates are days when your pass does not allow you entry into the parks. They do not apply on the day you buy your annual pass, but you cannot park-hop on the day you purchase an annual pass if it is a blackout date. There is a 20% family discount if buying five annual passes together.

How do I get my annual pass?
At the ticket booths, ask whether they can do an annual pass there and then - this is often available on quieter days of the week, and some weekends. Alternatively, ask if "Donald's Desk" is open. If so, follow the directions and complete the passport there.

If the desk is not open, you will buy a one-day ticket to Disneyland Park (not Walt Disney Studios Park). Once inside Disneyland Park, visit the "Bureau Pass Annuel" (located at the entrance of Discoveryland).

Here you will be asked for some details such as your address and name, have a photo taken for the card and have your annual pass made. The price of your day ticket will be deducted from your annual pass' price.

Allow about an hour for this process, as there may be a wait – the actual process itself takes less than 10 minutes. You must take a passport or ID card with you as proof of identity.

Please note: During Covid-19, ticket sales booths and the annual pass offices are currently closed. A dedicated desk is available at Walt Disney Studios Park. Call Disneyland Paris to verify this before your visit as this information may change.

Understanding the Parks

Before taking a detailed look at each of the theme parks, let us explain some of the must-knows, including parking, Disney Premier Access, character meets and much more.

Disney Premier Access

Disneyland Paris offers a paid skip-the-queue system called Disney Premier Access. If you use it, you can skip the regular queue and ride within minutes via a dedicated entrance.

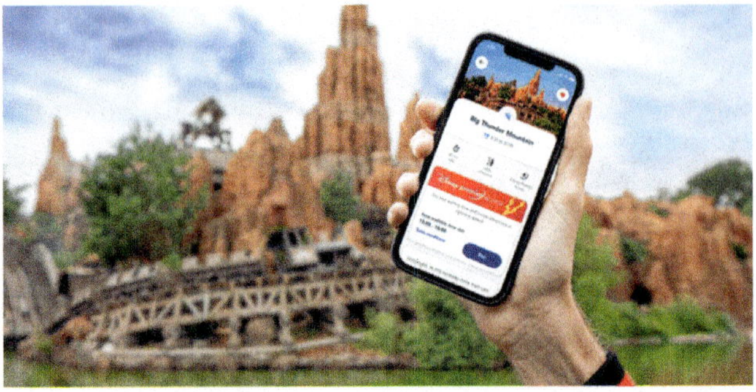

How do I use it?
The easiest way to use the system is to use the official Disneyland Paris app.

• **Step 1:** Download the official Disneyland Paris App and log in or create an account. Link your park tickets or hotel reservation.

• **Step 2:** When in the park, choose an attraction you would like to use Disney Premier Access on. Not all attractions are available.

• **Step 3:** You will be given a 1-hour time slot to return at - this will be the earliest available time. You cannot manually choose a different time slot. If this works for you, pay for your Disney Premier Access.

• **Step 4:** While waiting for your time slot, you can do something else such as shop, dine, watch a show or experience another attraction using the standby queue line.

• **Step 5:** Return at the selected time and enter via the dedicated Disney Premier Access ride entrance. Scan your QR code from the app and you'll be riding in minutes.

Do I need a smartphone?
If you don't have a smartphone, or don't want to use it, then you can purchase Disney Premier Access at Guest Services in either park.

How much does Disney Premier Access cost?
Price varies based on the attraction and how busy the park is. Each Disney Premier Access costs between €5 and €18 per person. It certainly isn't cheap.

What if the ride is having technical difficulties during my time slot?
A new QR code will be sent to you automatically at the end of your slot, or speak to a Cast Member at the ride entrance who can help you. You can wait to see if the attraction re-opens or use your new Pass to access the Disney Premier Access line for any other eligible attraction, at any time (no time slot).

Which attractions have Disney Premier Access available?
- *Big Thunder Mountain*
- *Phantom Manor*
- *Peter Pan's Flight*
- *Ratatouille: The Adventure*
- *Indiana Jones et le Temple du Péril*
- *Buzz Lightyear Laser Blast*
- *Orbitron: Machines Volantes*
- *Star Wars Hyperspace Mountain*
- *Star Tours: The Adventures continue*
- *The Twilight Zone Tower of Terror*
- *Autopia*

When Avengers Campus opens in summer 2022 we also expect to see the service at:

• Iron Man: Jukebox
• Web-Slingers: A Spider-Man Adventure

A rumour also states that *Crush's Coaster* may be getting Disney Premier Access in early 2022 although this had not been confirmed at the time of writing.

Will this really save me time?
Yes, due to the high price point, not everyone will use it. So, you can expect to gain near-instant access using Disney Premier Access. During less busy periods, it is probably not worth it.

Do children need Disney Premier Access to join the dedicated line?
Children under three do not need a Disney Premier Access to join the dedicated queue line. They must however be accompanied by an adult who has Disney Premier Access. All other children do each need a Disney Premier Access.

Can I buy as many Disney Premier Access as I want?
You may buy a maximum of 3 Disney Premier Access for each attraction for an individual guest each day, and up to 12 Disney Premier Access for a single attraction and time slot at a time, depending upon availability.

There are a limited number of Disney Premier Access available for each time slot.

What happened to Fastpass?
If you have previously visited Disneyland Paris and were familiar with the free Fastpass system, this has now been discontinued. Only the paid-for Disney Premier Access is available.

On-Ride Photos

Some of Disneyland Paris' most popular rides have cameras positioned and timed to take perfect on-ride photos of you at the most action-filled moments on attractions. Buy the photo and see yourself at the fastest, steepest, scariest and most fun moment of the ride. These make for timeless keepsakes.

When you exit selected rides, you will walk past screens that preview your photo (with a watermark on top). If you wish to purchase it, go to the photo counter.

You do not have to buy on-ride photos straight after your ride; you can pick them up at any time that same day. Just remember your unique number at the ride exit or ask a member of staff at the photo kiosk to write it down for you.

If you like the photo, Cast Members will show it to you up close before you pay for it. If you like it, buy it! You will treasure the photo for a long time.

Photo print prices start at €20 for one photo with a themed frame. A single photo without a frame is €17, and each additional photo costs €10.

Digital photos are also available via the PhotoPass+ system – more details on the following pages.

The attractions with on-ride photos are:
• *Big Thunder Mountain*
• *Pirates of the Caribbean*
• *Star Wars Hyperspace Mountain*
• *Buzz Lightyear Laser Blast*
• *The Twilight Zone: Tower of Terror.*

Top Tip: If you want photos from several rides, you can combine these on a PhotoPass. See our PhotoPass section on the following pages to find out how to save money on photos.

Disneyland Paris App

Disneyland Paris has a free iOS and Android app, which allows you to enhance your trip. With the app, you can plan your stay, including an overview of the hotels on offer, and a look at the different attractions throughout the resort. You can also create an itinerary and buy park tickets.

Once in the park, you can check the opening hours, book Table Service restaurants, see timings of shows and parades, and check the attraction wait times. It is this last feature that makes the app the most useful – no more walking to the wait time board on Main Street, U.S.A. You can check waits in the palm of your hand for both parks at the same time.

Finally, the app has recently been updated to allow you to pre-purchase/mobile order food and drink from some of the Quick Service restaurants, and book Disney Premier Access.

You will need a data connection to see live information, which means you must have data roaming enabled on your phone or you can use the free in-park Wi-Fi available to all guests.

PhotoPass

Disneyland Paris' PhotoPass is an easy to use system that makes collecting all your in-park photos easy.

Simply go to any in-park photographer (including those stationed at *Meet Mickey Mouse*, *Princess Pavilion: A Royal Invitation*, and with other characters) and after the photographer takes your photo, ask for a Disney PhotoPass.

Alternatively, you can ask for a PhotoPass card at any ride photo counter (this option is not advertised, but it is available if you ask).

Next time you have a photo taken, hand over your PhotoPass card and pictures will be added to it. You can do this throughout your visit and the photos will be kept together on the system. This card can be re-used throughout both parks anywhere you find a photographer or with on-ride photos.

Each photo is saved on the PhotoPass system for 7 days. Before your photos expire, visit one of these locations to view and purchase your photos: *New Century Notions: Flora's Unique Boutique* in Disneyland Park, *Walt Disney Studios Store* in Walt Disney Studios Park, and *The Disney Gallery* in Disney Village. You can also view the photos at the Disney shops at the on-site hotels.

At all these locations, you can purchase prints or digital versions of your PhotoPass photos. Multiple PhotoPass cards can be combined onto one account too.
The more photos you purchase, the lower the 'price per photo' becomes. You can also add an extra Disney touch with themed borders and details for free.

If you have used PhotoPass in the American parks, the Disneyland Paris system works similarly, but the prints are more reasonably priced at Disneyland Paris. Plus, there are fewer PhotoPass photographers throughout the parks in France.

PhotoPass+

Like the regular PhotoPass (covered on the previous page), PhotoPass+ allows you to collect ride and character photos, as well as photos in front of some iconic park locations. The difference here is that you pre-pay for an unlimited number of digital photos instead of paying for each print individually. PhotoPass+ costs €75 at the park.

PhotoPass+ includes a PhotoPass+ card and a lanyard to carry the card on. Plus, two mini cards are included, so that other members of your party can have their own card and easily add photos to the same account. This allows groups and families to split up and get pictures added to the same account easily.

Guests can add an unlimited number of photos to their account for 10 days following their PhotoPass+ activation.

To view photos, guests should create an online account at DisneyPhotoPass.eu.

Guests can view their photos on the DisneyPhotoPass.eu website and download them in high quality, as well as buy prints, photo books, calendars, gifts and more.

Photos stay on the PhotoPass+ website for one year after they are taken, giving you plenty of time to download your favourite images.

PhotoPass+ at Disneyland Paris is very similar to the 'Memory Maker' and Photopass system in the US parks – but on a smaller scale.

Guests who pre-book PhotoPass+ as part of their stay pay a reduced rate of €59. A PhotoPass+ voucher is given at check-in and is exchanged for the actual product at any shop in the parks that sells PhotoPass+.

Top Tip: Annual Pass discounts are available. Annual pass holders also get a PhotoPass+ card valid for one year from the date of purchase instead of just 10 days, offering fantastic value for money.

Rider Switch

Rider Switch is a time-saving solution that allows parents to reduce waiting times throughout their visit when riding attractions with height restrictions.

A common issue at theme parks is when two adults want to ride a thrill ride, but they have a child who is not tall enough to ride.

The solution is Disney's Rider Switch, which allows one adult to queue up and ride while the other stays with the child.

When the first adult reaches the end of the queue line, they ask for a Rider Switch pass. After riding, they give this pass to the second adult.

The second adult is then able to ride as soon as the first one returns. The second adult is granted near-immediate access to the ride, bypassing the entire regular queue line.

Each adult will experience the ride separately, but the second adult will not need to wait to ride.

Each attraction implements the system slightly differently, so ask the Cast Member at each ride entrance for details.

You do not need to have a child or baby present to use this service. You could use it to stay with an adult who does not wish to ride.

Single Rider

One of the best ways to significantly reduce your time waiting for attractions is to use the Single Rider queue instead of the regular standby queue. This is available at selected attractions at the resort.

The Single Rider queue fills free spaces on ride vehicles. For example, if a ride vehicle can seat 8 people and a group of 4 turns up, followed by a group of 3, then a Single Rider will fill the free space. This allows guests who are willing to ride with strangers to experience a shorter wait, and fills a space. This system reduces waits for everyone.

Single Rider queues may be closed when waits in that queue are too long, or when the theme park is not busy.

Single Rider Lines can be used by groups too, but each person in the group will be separated, and each person will ride in a different vehicle. You can, of course, wait for each other by the ride exit but you will not ride together.

The following attractions operate Single Rider Lines:
- *RC Racer*
- *Toy Soldier Parachute Drop*
- *Crush's Coaster*
- *Ratatouille: The Adventure*
- *Star Wars Hyperspace Mountain*
- *Indiana Jones et le Temple du Péril*

Larger Guests

Disneyland Paris has designed its attractions to be accessible to all guests, but sometimes a visitor's height or weight may limit the attractions they can visit for safety reasons.

At Disneyland Paris, unlike some other theme parks, there are no 'test seats' outside attractions. Therefore, if you are unsure whether you will be able to ride a particular attraction, it is best to speak to a Cast Member at the ride entrance.

You could also ask the Cast Member whether they could allow you to try sitting in the ride vehicle itself before queuing up.

Rides where larger guests may have difficulty include: *Star Wars Hyperspace Mountain, Indiana Jones et le Temple du Péril, Crush's Coaster* and *RC Racer* because of the restraints and limited legroom.

Orbitron and *Cars Quatre Roues Rallye* may also be a tight fit despite using seatbelt-style restraints.

Extra Magic Time

Extra Magic Time (previously Extra Magic Hours) allows selected guests early theme park access to selected attractions at both theme parks at Disneyland Paris for more than 1 hour each morning.

Guests get access to an almost empty park, ride with little to no wait and can meet Disney characters too. EMT includes most of the major rides at both theme parks.

Extra Magic Time (EMT) takes place at both theme parks daily from 8:30am to 9:30am. During less busy times of the year, only one of the two theme parks may be open for EMT. Check the Disneyland Paris calendar on the website for details.

Getting Extra Magic Time
The EMT benefit is available exclusively to guests staying at on-site Disney Hotels (not selected or partner hotels) and for guests who have a Magic Plus or Infinity Annual Pass, even if they are not staying at a Disney hotel.

Disney hotel guests will need their park tickets and their Magic Card (given at hotel check-in) to enter the parks during Extra Magic Time. Annual pass holders only need their annual pass.

What is open during EMT?
At Disneyland Park, selected attractions on Main Street, U.S.A., Discoveryland, Frontierland and Fantasyland are available - that's every land except Adventureland.

Typically, the following rides are available during Extra Magic Time – other rides and lands open at the official park opening time:
• *Dumbo: The Flying Elephant*
• *Peter Pan's Flight*
• *Lancelot's Carousel*
• *Mad Hatter's Teacups*
• *Princess Pavilion*
• *Meet Mickey Mouse*
• *Les Voyages de Pinocchio*
• *Buzz Lightyear Laser Blast*
• *Star Tours*
• *Hyperspace Mountain*
• *Orbitron*
• *Thunder Mesa Riverboat Landing*
• *Phantom Manor*
• *Big Thunder Mountain*.

Extra Magic Time at Walt Disney Studios Park typically includes the following attractions:
• *Crush's Coaster*
• *Cars Quatre Roues Rallye*
• *RC Racer*
• *Toy Soldiers Parachute Drop*
• *Slinky Dog Zig Zag Spin*
• *Flying Carpets Over Agrabah*
• *The Twilight Zone: Tower of Terror*
• *Ratatouille: The Adventure*.

Wheelchair and Pushchair Rentals

Wheelchair and pushchair rentals are available for guests who do not wish to bring their own.

If your child is recently out of a pushchair, it is often still worth renting one as it is likely they will get tired, due to the huge distances you will cover during a Disneyland Paris trip.

Sometimes it is nice just to let kids sit in their pushchair and have a break. Plus, they can also be used as an easy way to carry around bags.

It should be noted that Disneyland Paris' pushchairs do not recline, and do not have any real rain protection. Some people also say that the pushchairs are not the most comfortable.

The daily cost of hiring a wheelchair or pushchair is €25. The deposit required for a wheelchair is €200; it is €75 for a pushchair.

You are, of course, welcome to bring your own pushchair or wheelchair if you wish.

When experiencing attractions, be sure to leave your pushchair in the dedicated parking areas. Ask a Cast Member if you are not sure whether this is.

Pushchairs may be moved by Cast Members to keep them neat and organised.

Guided Tours

Note: Tours may be suspended due to Covid-19.

If you want to discover more about the magic behind Disneyland Paris' two theme parks, be sure to join one of the resort's guided tours. These tours are the perfect way to enhance your visit.

The Disneyland Park tour (duration: 2 hours) departs at 1:00pm or 2:00pm daily, and the Walt Disney Studios Park tour (duration: 90 minutes) departs at 3:00pm each day. The tour is available in the six official park languages, including English.

You will discover the work that goes into creating these parks, and find out secrets and see details that will wow you.

Additionally, *The Twilight Zone: Tower of Terror* tour goes into the details of the construction and design of The Hollywood Tower Hotel, as well as the references from *The Twilight Zone* TV show.

The Tower of Terror Tour is held in French only at 9:10am on Wednesdays and Saturdays.

Pricing for the theme park tours is €65 per adult and €45 for children ages 3 to 11 inclusive. The Tower of Terror tour is €50 and €34. Reservations can be made by emailing Disney Special Activities at dlp.disney.special.activities@disney.com.

Disney Shopping Service

The Disney Shopping Service allows you to buy an item at any of the theme park shops and pick it up later.

When paying for your goods before 3:00pm, ask to use the Disney Shopping Service. You will leave the item with the Cast Member who served you. When you have finished your day at the park, you can pick up your shopping.

You can either pick up your purchases at the World of Disney store in Disney Village from 6:00pm, or at the Disney boutiques at on-site Disney hotels or selected partner hotels from 8:00pm.

This means that you can collect all your items in one spot, even if you have multiple items from different shops. This service allows you to be free to eat, shop, ride attractions and watch shows to your heart's content without carrying your shopping around.

Lockers

There are two staffed luggage services located to the right of the theme park turnstiles.

There is also an external automatic left luggage storage facility on the upper level of *Marne-La-Vallee – Chessy* train station.

Storage at the parks and in the station range in price from €5 to €10 depending on the size and the number of bags stored.

For the station lockers, you need the exact change (there is a change machine inside the locker room). At the Disney Parks storage facilities, you can pay by cash or by card.

Infinity Annual Pass holders may store one item at the park storage at no cost.

You can access the Disneyland Paris storage as many times as you want throughout the day for one set daily fee.

With the station lockers, every time you open the lockers, you must pay again to lock them. Plus, you must go back and forth through the Disneyland Paris security checkpoint each time to access the station lockers.

Meeting the Disney Characters

For many visitors, meeting characters is the highlight of their trip. Playing with Pluto, talking to Cinderella and hugging Mickey makes for magical memories.

COVID-19 Changes: At the moment guests are meeting characters at a distance at 'selfie spots' and cannot hug them or get too close.

Disneyland Park:
Characters are scheduled to appear around the park throughout the day. Please note that characters may meet at different locations than those shown here.

Mickey is at *Meet Mickey Mouse* in Fantasyland, and the Disney princesses can be seen at *Princess Pavilion* (also in Fantasyland).

Near *Alice's Curious Labyrinth*, you will find Alice and her friends, including The Mad Hatter and Tweedle Dum and Dee. Also nearby, you can meet Winnie the Pooh and Friends.

By Casey's Corner, you can see Donald and friends, whereas, by the *Liberty Arcade*, you can find Minnie and friends.

Woody and Friends are by *Cowboy Cookout Restaurant*, Baloo can be found by *Hakuna Matata Restaurant* in Adventureland, and Chip and Dale are near *Colonel Hathi's Pizza Outpost*.

Elsewhere in Adventureland, you can expect to see Peter Pan and friends by *Pirate's Beach*, and Aladdin and friends near *Agrabah Café*.
At *Starport* in Discoveryland, you can meet Darth Vader.

If there is a specific character you would like to see, ask at City Hall (on Town Square) whether they have a schedule for them. Not all characters are available to meet daily.

You can also have a Disney princess dining experience at *L'Auberge de Cendrillon* (€77 per adult, €45 per child - temporarily closed during Covid-19).

You are also able to meet Disney characters at Plaza Gardens on Main Street, U.S.A for breakfast (suspended during Covid-19).

Characters usually stop meeting in both parks by mid-afternoon. Check the in-park schedule for details.

Walt Disney Studios Park:
You will find many characters in the Toon Studio area of the park to the left of *Crush's Coaster* at permanent outdoor photo locations. Here you will often find Mickey, Minnie, Buzz Lightyear, Woody and other characters. Check the app for exact character appearances.

At *Animation Celebration*, you can meet Olaf from Frozen.

Hotels:
Characters are present at on-site hotels in the morning at breakfast time. Guests staying at the *Hotel New York - Art of Marvel* can also meet Spider-Man at a photo location

Classic characters such as Mickey, Minnie, Tigger, Chip and Dale and Donald Duck are also present during the character meals at *Inventions* restaurant in the Disneyland Hotel.

Lunch and Dinner meals at *Inventions* are €70 for adults, and €40 for kids. *Inventions* also hosts a themed brunch on Sundays priced at €99 adults, €45 kids, from 1:00pm to 3:00pm – you can book both meals even if you are not staying at this hotel.

Please note *Disneyland Hotel* is closed for refurbishment throughout 2022.

How to Spend Less time Queuing

Disneyland Paris meticulously themes its queues to introduce an attraction's story before you board. However, no one likes waiting, and we all want to get on a ride as quickly as possible. Visiting a theme park will always involve some waiting but in this chapter, we cover our top tips on minimising this.

1 - Eat outside of typical dining hours

At Disneyland Paris, whether you want to eat at a Table Service restaurant or a Quick Service meal, waiting for your food is part of the game. Have lunch before midday or after 3:00pm for much shorter waits. Have dinner before 7:00pm to reduce your wait times. A wait of 45 minutes or longer just to order is relatively typical at peak times at Quick Service restaurants.

2 - Quick Service meal tricks

At Quick Service locations, cashiers have two queues, and alternate between them – count how many groups (families) are in front of you in the queue. There may be ten people in front of you in one queue line but only two families. The other queue line may have five people but from five different families. The queue with ten people will move more quickly with only two orders to process versus the other queue's five orders.

New: The Disneyland Paris app now also allows you to preorder your meal and collect it at a specific time at Café Hyperion and Casey's Corner. We expect this to be rolled out to other Quick Service restaurants in the future. This is a great time-saver.

3 - On-site Disney Hotel guests

If you are staying at an on-site Disneyland Paris hotel or have an annual pass with this benefit, take advantage of Extra Magic Time. You get entry into the theme parks over one hour before regular guests do. During this time, you can experience many of the park's attractions with minimal waits. See our Extra Magic Time section on page 35 for more details.

4 - Disneyland Park opens early

Disneyland Park's opening hours usually say it officially opens at 10:00am, but you can enter the park 30 minutes earlier. This means you can enjoy the atmosphere, eat breakfast, start shopping and take photos on Main Street, U.S.A. and of Sleeping Beauty Castle. In front of the castle, the entrances to all the lands will be cordoned off by Cast Members until the park's official opening time.

If you are a Disney hotel guest or a Magic Plus or Infinity annual pass holder, show your Magic Card or annual pass, and you can enter Fantasyland, Discoveryland and Frontierland as part of Extra Magic Time. Otherwise, wait by the ropes at the entrances of the lands for "rope-drop" as the park opens. If you are there before the park opens, you can be on your first ride in minutes.

5 - Walt Disney Studios Park opens early

Walt Disney Studios Park also opens at 9:30am instead of the official 10:00am opening time advertised. At that time, you can walk around the entire park, and most attractions will be open as Extra Magic Time starts at 8:30am. Some attractions will only open at 10:00am at the official park opening time. We recommend going straight to ride *Crush's Coaster* or *Ratatouille, or* when Avenger's Campus opens, one of the two rides there.

6 - Skip the parades and fireworks

If you have already seen the parades, shows or fireworks, use that time to experience rides as the wait times are often much shorter during these big events. If you have not seen the park's entertainment offerings before, we do *not* recommend you skip them. Parades and shows are only performed at set times of the day and most of these are just as much a part of the Disney theme park experience as the rides.

7 - Ride outdoor attractions while it rains

Outdoor attractions such as *Dumbo, Flying Carpets over Agrabah, Casey Junior, Storybook Canal boats, Big Thunder Mountain, Indiana Jones et le Temple du Peril, Lancelot's Carousel (outdoor queue), Slinky Dog Zigzag Spin, Toy Soldiers Parachute Drop* and *RC Racer* have much-reduced waits when it is raining. Yes, you may get wet while riding (a jacket may help) but the wait times *will* be shorter too.

Top Tip: Many guests return to the hotels when it rains, so many of the indoor rides may also have shorter queues during inclement weather.

8 - Choose when to visit carefully

Visit during an off-peak time if possible. If you are visiting on New Year's Day, expect to queue a lot longer than on a Tuesday in the middle of January. Seasonal events such as Christmas and Halloween also draw bigger crowds.

Of course, weekends are busier than weekdays. See our 'When to Visit' section (page 5) to make the most of your time.

9 - Shop at the start or end of the day

If you enter the park during the pre-opening period from 9:30am to 10:00am, this is a perfect time to go shopping. Alternatively, go shopping at the end of the day. Even when the park is 'officially' closed, the shops on Main Street, U.S.A. stay open up to an hour longer than the rest of the park. Alternatively, walk over to Disney Village in the evening, and go shopping there until much later in the evening - until midnight during peak times!

Additionally, on-site hotels and some partner hotels have a small Disney boutique inside them. Do not waste your time during the day shopping, do it at strategic times and make the most of your time in the parks.

10 - Download the Official Disneyland Paris App

Disneyland Paris' smartphone app contains all kinds of information from the wait times for the rides, to the timings of parades, shows, character appearances and more. As such, you will not waste time crossing the park to find out that a character you saw earlier in the day has now left a particular location, or that a ride is closed for technical difficulties. Plus you can book restaurant reservations and order meals ahead of time.

Dining

There are a variety of places to eat at Disneyland Paris. Food options vary from sandwich and snack locations to Quick Service (fast food) places, character buffets, Table Service dining and even fine dining options. Eating can be as much a part of the experience as the attractions at Disneyland Paris.

Making Reservations

If you want to guarantee you will be able to dine at a specific restaurant, it is worth booking a table in advance.

You can make your restaurant reservation up to 60 days in advance but, in reality, booking even two weeks or less beforehand will usually get you a table at most places.

Most people do not book restaurants in theme parks in Europe far in advance, which is a stark change from the American Disney parks.

Despite this, it is worth making a reservation as early as possible if you want a meal on a specific day. You will also be seated much more quickly with a reservation than without one.

Purchasing a meal plan does not guarantee you a table in a restaurant, so be sure to make a restaurant reservation in advance if there is a particular place you want to dine.

The easiest way to make a reservation is to use the official Disneyland Paris app. You can also browse all the restaurant menus and see pricing here.

Alternatively, you can call the Dining Reservation hotline on +33 (0)1 60 30 40 50 and book in several languages, including English.

You can also book at City Hall in Disneyland Park, Studio Services in Walt Disney Studios or at any of the Disney hotel lobbies.

Finally, you can visit any of the restaurants and book directly.

You do not need to be staying in a Disney hotel to book a table at a restaurant - anyone visiting the theme parks can do this. If you cannot attend a reservation, it is good practice to cancel it as early as possible.

In the low season, it is possible to make reservations for the same day or the next day. In the high season, restaurants are fully booked a week or more in advance.

Top Tip: If you wish to dine at *Auberge de Cendrillon* (princess character dining - currently suspended due to Covid-19), specifically, it is worth booking as soon as reservations open - it is very popular.

Meal Plans

The Meal Plan system is currently undergoing a radical overhaul. Therefore, this information is valid for arrivals starting 31st March 2022.

Meal Plans allow you to pre-purchase meal credits so that on arrival at the resort, you do not need to worry about the cost of meals.

Meal plan entitlements are digitally loaded onto your Magic Card which is given when checking in at your hotel.

Meal Plans are only available to guests who book packages with an official Disney Hotel and park tickets.

All Half-Board Meal Plans include (per night):
• One Breakfast at your hotel
• One Table Service, Quick Service or Buffet meal for lunch or dinner.

The Full-Board *Standard* Meal Plan includes (per night):
• Breakfast at your hotel
• One Quick Service meal
• One Table Service or Buffet meal

The Full-Board *Plus* Meal Plan includes (per night):
• Breakfast at your hotel
• Two Quick Service, Table Service or Buffet meals
• An extra meal (lunch or dinner) on your last day.

The Full-Board *Extra Plus* Meal Plan includes (per night):
• Breakfast at your hotel
• Two Quick Service, Table Service or Buffet meals (one meal per *stay* can be a character meal at *Auberge de Cendrillon* or *Café Mickey* at no extra charge)
• An extra meal (lunch or dinner) on your last day.
• One Snack and Drink (typically a pastry plus drink)
• One Drink (alcoholic or non-alcoholic).

Standard and Plus Meal Plans are valid at 31 restaurants at the resort. Extra Plus Meal Plans are valid at 33 restaurants.

A meal voucher includes a set menu or buffet, and one soft drink.

Occasionally, Disneyland Paris runs promotions with free Meal Plans included with package bookings.

If you eat at a restaurant that is not included in your Meal Plan, you can use your vouchers for a discount. E.g. If you have a 'Standard' voucher, but visit an 'Extra Plus' restaurant, the 'Standard' voucher's value is deducted from your bill, and you pay the difference. Meal Plans can save you up to 15% off the menu prices, although this varies based on what you eat. For many guests, the peace of mind of pre-paid meals is the best part of the deal.

Meals are from a set menu on all meal plans - you do not get access to the full a la carte menu. At a buffet, all items are available. If in doubt, ask your waiter before ordering.

The Half Board plans include one voucher per night for any restaurant from the grid on the next page; the Full Board plans include two vouchers per night for restaurants of your choice from the grid. Breakfast is also included in both plans. Breakfast is an extra charge for guests without meal plans.

Meal Plan vouchers are accepted at all Disney Park and Disney Hotel restaurants and in some Disney Village restaurants (apart from *McDonald's, Planet Hollywood, Rainforest Cafe, King Ludwig Castle, Starbucks, Earl of Sandwich, Five Guys* and *Vapiano*).

Pricing:
Prices are below and are per night of a stay.

For arrivals from 31st March 2022

	Standard Adult	Standard Child	Plus Adult	Plus Child	Extra Plus Adult	Extra Plus Child
Half Board	€49	€30	€59	€40	N/A	N/A
Full Board	€69	€40	€89	€55	€119	€75

The Standard Meal Plan is only available at *Disney's Davy Crockett Ranch* and *Hotel Santa Fe.*

For arrivals from 31st March 2022

Restaurant Name	Restaurant Type	Location	On Standard Plan?	On Plus Plan?	On Extra Plus Plan?
Agrabah Cafe	Buffet	Disneyland Park	Yes	Yes	Yes
Annette's Diner	Table Service	Disney Village	Yes	Yes	Yes
Auberge de Cendrillon	Character Dining	Disneyland Park	No	No	Yes
Beaver Creek Tavern	Table Service	Sequoia Lodge Hotel	Yes	Yes	Yes
Bistrot Chez Remy	Table Service	Walt Disney Studios Park	Yes	Yes	Yes
Café Mickey	Character Dining	Disney Village	No	No	Yes
Cape Cod	Buffet	Newport Bay Club Hotel	Yes	Yes	Yes
Captain Jack's	Table Service	Disneyland Park	Yes	Yes	Yes
Chuck Wagon Cafe	Buffet	Hotel Cheyenne	Yes	Yes	Yes
Crockett's Tavern	Buffet	Davy Crockett's Ranch	Yes	Yes	Yes
Downtown Restaurant	Buffet	Disney's Hotel New York - Art of Marvel	Yes	Yes	Yes
Hunter's Grill	Buffet	Sequoia Lodge Hotel	Yes	Yes	Yes
La Cantina	Buffet	Santa Fe Hotel	Yes	Yes	Yes
La Grange at Billy Bob's	Table Service	Disney Village	Yes	Yes	Yes
Plaza Gardens	Buffet	Disneyland Park	Yes	Yes	Yes
Silver Spur Steakhouse	Table Service	Disneyland Park	Yes	Yes	Yes
The Lucky Nugget Saloon	Hybrid Service	Disneyland Park	Yes	Yes	Yes
The Steakhouse	Table Service	Disney Village	Yes	Yes	Yes
Walt's: An American Restaurant	Table Service	Disneyland Park	Yes	Yes	Yes
Yacht Club	Table Service	Newport Bay Club Hotel	Yes	Yes	Yes

Vouchers from all meal plans are also valid all Quick Service restaurants throughout the two theme parks.

Top Places to Eat

Here are recommended dining locations at both theme parks - there are a mix of Quick Service and Table Service locations. We list these in no particular order.

The Steakhouse - Located in Disney Village, this Table Service location has hands-down the best steaks on property. Delicious food and a great atmosphere make this a solid choice for any evening.

Bistrot Chez Remy - This is the only Table Service option in Walt Disney Studios Park. The menu is very limited so do check it beforehand, but if the food is to your liking, then this is one of the best themed and most 'fun' restaurants throughout the resort.

The Lucky Nugget Saloon - Located in Frontierland in Disneyland Park. This restaurant has changed its dining concept several times, so who knows what it might be when you visit? It is a Quick Service restaurant but the food is delivered to your table. Sometimes shows play on the stage here too.

Restaurant Hakuna Matata - Perhaps the best Quick Service location in Disneyland Paris with more unique options than your standard burgers and fries that are found throughout a lot of the theme parks.

Plaza Gardens - Our go-to option when we fancy a buffet. The selection is vast and the setting is great; with the right table, you may even be able to spy the park's iconic castle.

Tipping in Restaurants

In France, a 15% service charge is included in your meal price, although this may not be itemised in the bill.

You are not expected to leave any additional money for service.

If you particularly liked the service, free to leave a few Euros in cash as a tip. A 5% to 10% tip is more than enough, although French guests rarely leave a tip.

Sometimes in France, waiters will not return with your change and will assume it is their tip; if this was not your intention, let them know. This is much less common at Disneyland Paris than elsewhere. One way to avoid this is to always pay by card.

Good to Know

• For buffets, kids' prices apply for ages 3 to 11 inclusive.
• You may have the option of breakfast at Plaza Gardens in Disneyland Park for €25 per person. Ask at reception for the availability of this experience if you do not book in advance.
• Adults can order from the kids' menu at Quick Service locations. At Table Service locations, this is at the discretion of the Cast Member serving you.
• For an idea of how much food costs at the restaurants, see our parks chapters which list set menu prices and a la carte main courses.
• All restaurants should have at least one vegan option, but Cast Members and chefs will do their best to accommodate you. Making a reservation and stating your dietary requirements helps.

Breakfast Pricing

Breakfast is not included with hotel reservations. Unless you purchase a meal plan, you will need to pay for breakfast separately.

These are the breakfast prices per person per night:
• **Davy Crockett Ranch** - €12 adult or child
• **Santa Fe & Cheyenne** - €24 per adult, €17 per child
• **Sequoia Lodge** - €24 per adult, €17 per child
• **Newport Bay Club & Hotel New York (The Art of Marvel)** - €28 per adult, €23 per child
• **Disneyland Hotel** (hotel currently closed) - €36 per adult, €27 per child

To eat breakfast in the park at Plaza Gardens with Disney characters, the full price is €41 per adult and €35 per child - guests with a meal plan simply pay the difference. Breakfast with the Princesses at *L'Auberge de Cendrillon* is €49 per adult and €39 per child.

Please note character dining is currently suspended.

Restaurant Types:

Buffet – All-you-can-eat locations where you fill your plate from the food selection as often as you want. Buffets may or may not include a drink.

Quick Service – Fast food. Look at the menus, pay for your food and collect it a few minutes later. You will find everything from burgers and chips, to chicken, pizza and pasta. Be aware that Disney 'fast'-food locations are notoriously slow and a queue of just four or five people in front of you can easily be a wait time of 20 to 30 minutes.

Table Service – Order from a menu. A waiter brings the food to your table.

Character Dining – *(Unavailable during COVID-19)* Characters interact with you and take photos as you eat. We expect this to return in 2022.

Top Tip: Whether it be a snack cart, a Quick Service location or a Table Service restaurant, you are never obliged to order from a set menu. Ordering specific items 'a la carte' is completely fine, although it may save you money if you order certain set menu combinations.

Disneyland Park

Disneyland Park is the main theme park at Disneyland Paris. It is made up of five lands filled with fantasy, adventure and excitement.

Disneyland Park, also known as *Parc Disneyland* in French, is based on the original Disneyland that opened in California in 1955. Every Disney resort around the world has one of these classic "Magic Kingdom-style" Disney parks. The park spans 140 acres, which is almost twice the size of the original.

Disneyland Park is the most visited theme park in Europe and the thirteenth most visited in the world, with 9.8 million visitors in 2019. The park has plenty to offer guests with almost fifty attractions (rides, themed areas and shows), as well as character experiences, dining options and plenty of places to shop.

Disneyland Park is commonly called the most beautiful Disney theme park in the world.

The park is divided into five areas (or "lands") around Sleeping Beauty Castle in the centre. These are Main Street USA, Frontierland, Adventureland, Fantasyland and Discoveryland. Each land has its own overarching theme, with a unique soundtrack, décor, costumes and themed attractions. Around the edges of the park, you will find the Disneyland Railroad, which transports guests between these different lands.

As queuing is inevitable at theme parks, to help you determine how long you may wait to experience the attractions, we have included "average wait times"; these are for peak times such as school holidays (Summer, Christmas, Easter) and weekends throughout the year. Wait times outside busy times are often lower.

COVID-19 CHANGES:
Face coverings are required for guests ages 6 and up at all times at the parks except when eating. Some offerings may be reduced or suspended.

Is Disney Premier Access available?	Minimum height (in metres)
Is there an On-Ride Photo?	Attraction Length
Average wait times (on peak days)	

Main Street, U.S.A.

Main Street, U.S.A. is the entrance to Disneyland Park, taking you to Sleeping Beauty Castle and beyond.

Main Street, U.S.A. is the entrance area of Disneyland Park, leading you towards *Sleeping Beauty Castle*. It is themed to look like 1920s America.

Main Street, U.S.A. has many shops on both sides of the street, the king of which is the **Emporium** where you are sure to find something to buy!

There are places to eat up and down the street too, including Quick Service and Table Service restaurants, as well as snack locations. There are also other food shops and carts around Main Street, U.S.A.

Before entering Main Street, U.S.A. itself, you will see Town Square with a gazebo in the centre.

City Hall is immediately to the left on Town Square; this is "Guest Services". Ask any questions you have here. They can also make reservations for tours and restaurants, and accept complaints and positive feedback too.

For disabled guests, an accessibility card is available at City Hall providing easier access to attractions. See our 'Guests with Disabilities' chapter on page 83 for more information on this.

Running parallel to Main Street, U.S.A. are the **Liberty Arcade** and **Discovery Arcade**. These provide an alternative covered route through the park, which is especially useful when it is raining or when a parade or the fireworks are on. The Disney Imagineers learnt a valuable lesson from the other Disney theme parks, where Main Street, U.S.A. often became congested throughout the day.

You will often find character meet and greets in this area of the park, as well as live music.

Top Tip: As you walk up Main Street, U.S.A. listen to the sounds from the windows on the first floor to hear the noise that the town's residents make. You can hear a dentist in one window, a man taking a bath in another and even a piano recital!

Dining Key:
€ (Under €15)
€€ (€16 to €29)
€€€ (€30 to €39)
€€€€ (€40 to €49)
€€€€€ (€50+)

Prices relate to set menus for one person where available.

The in-park restaurants accept all meal plans, except *Auberge de Cendrillon* which only accepts the Extra Plus Meal Plan. Learn more about Meal Plans on page 41.

Disneyland Railroad - Main Street, U.S.A. Station

Take a grand tour of Disneyland Park onboard an authentic steam train. Whether you use it as a form of transportation or just a way of seeing the sights, the Disneyland Railroad is a fun way to enjoy the park. You even get to peek inside *Pirates of the Caribbean* along the route.

A full trip around the park takes about 20 minutes.

This attraction usually stops operating several hours before the park closes (and also temporarily during the daily parade).

Main Street Vehicles and Horse-Drawn Street Cars

What better way to see Main Street, U.S.A. than from a vehicle – whether it is a horse-drawn car, a double-decker bus or one of the other modes of transport.

These vehicles typically only operate in the morning, and you simply wait for the next vehicle to turn up at designated spots on Town Square and on Central Plaza in front of the park's iconic castle - look out for the lampposts that have a sign saying 'City Vehicle Stop.'

Throughout the day, at unannounced times, the fountains in the moat of Sleeping Beauty Castle come to life, along with music, for special two to three-minute happenings. This takes place eight times per day but no schedule is officially published. If you are there on the hour or at half past the hour, you are more likely to see these happening.

These fountain shows change with the seasons, and have seasonal variations during Halloween, Christmas and St. Patrick's Day, for example.

Dining

Walt's Restaurant (€€€€ to €€€€€) – Table Service with French and international food. A vegan set menu is available.
Casey's Corner – (€) Counter Service. Serves ballgame themed snacks. Classic hot dogs - €9.50; 8-piece chicken nuggets - €9; salad - €7; desserts - €2 to €4; hot and cold drinks - €3.30 to €3.70; brownie and hot drink deal - €5.60; beer - €5.90. In-app mobile order is available at Casey's Corner.
Plaza Gardens (€€€) – Buffet. A character breakfast is available here for €41 per adult and €35 per child. The buffet is currently suspended due to Covid-19 and this is operating as a Table Service location instead
Victoria's Home-Style Restaurant (€) – Counter Service. Hot and cold drinks €3 to €6.50. Serves milkshakes in warmer months. Serves Mickey Waffles seasonally - €9.
Market House Deli (€) – Counter Service and Snacks. Serves sandwiches and coffees.
Cookie Kitchen and Cable Car Bake Shop (€) – Counter Service for Cable Car Bake Shop and take-away for Cookie Kitchen. Serves cookies, muffins and pastries as well as drinks.
The Gibson Girl Ice Cream Parlour (€) – Take-away only ice cream location. May also serve Mickey Waffles especially during colder months. Ice creams are €4 to €5.

Frontierland

Step into Frontierland and be transported to the Wild Western town of Thunder Mesa.

In addition to the attractions featured on the following pages, you may also wish to visit **Rustler Roundup Shootin' Gallery** where you can practice your shooting skills in a carnival-style game. There is an additional charge for this attraction. Other attractions in this land include the **Disneyland Railroad's Frontierland Station**, and **Pocahontas Indian Village** - a themed outdoor playground.

Big Thunder Mountain

According to the Disney legend, Big Thunder Mountain and the town of Thunder Mesa were discovered in the late 1800s.

In the town, a train line was constructed to transport ore around the mountain. However, the town was cursed, and it was soon struck by an earthquake.

Residents left the town, but a few years later the trains were found driving themselves around the mountain.

Guests can now take a 4-minute ride in one of these mine trains for themselves.

Along the way, you will see collapsing bridges, experience a dynamite blast, see bats and much more on this wild ride!

Yes | 1.02m | Yes | 4 mins | 60 to 90 mins

Most of the action takes place on an island in the middle of the lake, making it a unique version of the ride compared to other Disney theme parks around the world.

It is also the longest, tallest and fastest of the Big Thunder Mountain rides, but it is easily the most kid-friendly of Disneyland Paris' roller coasters.

At the end, you have the option of buying your on-ride photo if you wish.

This is one of our favourite attractions in the park and should not be missed.

Lion King: Rhythms of the Pride Lands

See this West End theatre-style production of the Lion King. In this 30-minute show, you'll be dazzled by acrobats, dancers and live singers.

Entry into the show is free, but we recommend arriving at least 45 minutes before show time (check the app for showtimes) as seats are limited.

Alternatively, you can pay €15 in the Disneyland Paris app to book a seat in advance and guarantee entry - even with this, we'd still recommend turning up 30 minutes before showtime for the best seat.

Phantom Manor

Yes | None | No | 7 mins | Less than 30 mins

Phantom Manor is a must-see attraction: the atmosphere, music, and details are amongst the best in the whole resort.

Phantom Manor is a theme ride. It is not a horror-maze attraction with actors jumping out to scare you, and as there is no minimum height restriction, the attraction is accessible to all ages. However, do be wary of frightening younger kids.

After a walk-through section in the manor's lobby and other rooms introduces the story, you'll sit in "doombuggies" for the ride portion of the attraction. These rotate and tilt to show you parts of the manor as they travel through it.

You can expect to see pianos playing by themselves, door knockers that have a mind of their own, a seance, and ghosts gathering for a ballroom dance.

Throughout the attraction, there are no jump-out scares, but the initial walk-through section may frighten some children due to the effects used here, and the dark. The animatronics in the cemetery scene may also frighten young children. These all pass by relatively quickly, and for every scarier moment there is a fun moment.

If you are unsure whether your child will be comfortable with the ride, try doing it during the daytime when the building's exterior looks less imposing. You could also try watching an on-ride video online before visiting to see if it is suitable.

If you are unsure of whether your kids will enjoy it, we recommend *not* making this your first ride as riding this at the start of a trip can make kids apprehensive of all other rides - even if they are very different.

We highly recommend making a stop at this ride as it is a true Disney classic, and as the ride's main character Melanie says: "Be sure to bring your death certificate. We're just dying to have you."

The storyline of this attraction is unique, despite similar Haunted Mansion-style rides existing at other Disney parks worldwide.

Phantom Manor has a dark storyline: on her wedding day, Melanie Ravenswood eagerly awaited her groom, not knowing that a phantom haunted the house she was in. The phantom (Melanie's father) lured the groom into the attic and hanged him. Melanie waited for her groom, but he never turned up. Now, she roams around the manor still in her wedding dress. Today, you venture through this derelict manor as you discover Melanie's story.

Thunder Mesa Riverboat Landing

☆ No | None | 15 minutes | Less than 30 minutes

Set sail on a classic riverboat around *Big Thunder Mountain* and admire Frontierland's scenery. The riverboat is a relaxing change of pace from the crowds in the park and there is plenty of space to roam around the boat.

There is some limited seating and you can listen to the story of the Molly Brown riverboat on the speakers as you sail along the river, though the audio is not particularly loud - most people just take in the atmosphere.

Top Tip: The Riverboat's operating hours are shorter than many other attractions. It typically closes in the middle of the afternoon or early evening.

There's More to Frontierland Than Meets The Eye

As well as the major attractions featured here, you should enjoy the little details that make Frontierland unique. As you walk into Frontierland from Central Plaza, stop by **Fort Comstock**, the timber-themed entrance to the land. Notice the little details here, and if the steps are open on the left, climb up for a different perspective on this part of the park.

Phantom Manor has its own cemetery at the exit called **Boot Hill**. When you come out of the attraction, you can turn right down the hill to the front of the manor or continue straight ahead to Boot Hill. This area contains tombstones of several Thunder Mesa residents, which all tell their own story through gags and rhymes. You can also access Boot Hill without riding *Phantom Manor* by walking up the hill to the right of the manor.

Even the restaurants and shops are filled with details. **The Lucky Nugget Saloon** hosts live music and other acts. **Cowboy Cookout BBQ** also has live music, and the Imagineers went to town with the theming. Notice the chairs, for example - unlike other restaurants where everything is uniform, here there are many different types and styles of chairs because in the Wild West the townsfolk would bring chairs from home.

Dining

Silver Spur Steakhouse (€€€ to €€€€) – Table Service. Steakhouse and grill.
The Lucky Nugget Saloon (€€) – Counter Service serving American fare.
Cowboy Cookout Barbecue (€) – Counter Service serving Tex-Mex and BBQ food.
Fuente del Oro (€ to €€) – Counter Service serving Tex-Mex fare.
Last Chance Cafe (€) – Counter Service. Take-away snack meals such as vegan chilli 'con carne' and chicken wings. Also sells desserts, beer, hot and cold drinks.

Adventureland

Venture into an Arabian story, the Caribbean or a temple with Indiana Jones.

In addition to the attractions covered below, you may also want to check out **Adventure Isle** (a walkthrough area with winding paths, caves, a pirate ship, and a suspension bridge), **Le Passage Enchanté d'Aladdin** (a walkthrough attraction with scenes from the story of *Aladdin*) and **La Plage des Pirates** (an outdoor playground).

Indiana Jones et le Temple du Peril

Yes | 1.40m | No | 2 mins | 25 to 45 mins

This rollercoaster will take you on an archaeological adventure through the lost Temple of Doom.

Your adventure will have you climbing in search of treasure, dropping and turning around tight corners, and meandering in and around the Temple. You will even descend rapidly into a 360-degree loop as your mine cart goes 'out of control'.

The ride has the biggest minimum-height limit of any ride at any Disney park worldwide – 140cm. It was also the first Disney rollercoaster in the world to go upside down. The ride even ran backwards for a few years, but now runs forward once again.

This is one of the most intense coasters at the resort with the loop being particularly tight. It is also quite a rough ride.

Of all the coasters in the park, this ride usually has the shortest queue as it is hidden at the back of the park, and the minimum height limit means it is off-limits to most kids under the age of 10. Overall, it is a relatively short but fun experience.

Top Tip 1: Although this attraction does sometimes get long wait times, it is almost always deserted after the daily parade.

Top Tip 2: This attraction offers a Single Rider queue.

Pirates of the Caribbean

No | None | Yes | 10 mins | 15 to 45 mins

Ahoy me hearties! Set sail through the world of *Pirates of the Caribbean* at Disneyland Paris.

Board a boat and enjoy a ten-minute journey into a fort invaded by pirates. You'll float by scenes with amazing audio-animatronic characters bringing the action to life.

It may just be the best-themed attraction in all of Disneyland Park. The attention to detail is fantastic, from the queue line to the Cast Members' costumes and the music to the sets.

Your boat will go down two short drops, so be warned - *ye may get wet!*

This attraction is based on the original *Pirates of the Caribbean* ride in Disneyland in California. *Pirates of the Caribbean* was the final ride Walt Disney himself supervised the creation of at Disneyland.

The ride now also includes some well-known film characters including Jack Sparrow, Blackbeard and Barbossa.

Be aware that the queue line for the ride is not well lit due to the atmosphere it aims to create, and therefore it is very dark. This will especially strike you when riding during the daytime as your eyes take a while to adjust, so watch your step and hold onto your children's hands in the queue line.

Each of the boats can take 23 passengers so the queue is almost always moving, but it is also an extremely popular ride. This means that although most of the year wait times stay below 20 minutes, on peak days, you may see these rise to 60 minutes. In the indoor section, there is a lot to see even as you wait - as we've said before, the attention to detail is amazing.

The recommended minimum age for this attraction is 12 months old as it is dark and loud.

This is a must-see, family-friendly ride that is a classic Disney experience.

Warning: As the queue line for this attraction is so dark and there are so many people in one place, sadly it is a favourite spot for pickpockets – especially when there are long waits. Be aware of your surroundings and keep an eye on your belongings.

La Cabane des Robinson

Enter the world of Swiss Family Robinson as you explore the treehouse made from the wood of their shipwreck. You can see the complex water wheel system that they built to get water up to the bedrooms, and explore the kitchen, living rooms and bedrooms.

No | None | No | 5 mins | None

This is a walkthrough experience and kids love exploring and climbing the steps.

From the top, the view is mostly obscured by the tree's leaves, but you can get an interesting perspective on the park from up here.

Adventureland is designed to be explored on foot...

Of all the lands at Disneyland Park, Adventureland is the one that appears to have the smallest number of attractions. However, this area of the park is filled with incredible details that you need to find for yourself outside of the main attractions.

Adventureland is built around Adventure Isle, with *La Cabane des Robinson* at the centre. As well as the treehouse, be sure to step aboard the **Pirate Galleon** moored in the centre of the land, and explore the caves under the treehouse to see the secrets that lie here. There are also a separate set of **caves** next to the galleon - here you will find treasure, skeletons and cascading waterfalls.

Follow the signs to **"Pont Suspendu"** to reach Spyglass Hill and enjoy the stunning view over the park. Don't forget to cross the wobbly Suspension Bridge and the Floating Bridge (**"Pont Flotant"**) which is right next to the Swiss Family Robinson's shipwreck.

Dining

Agrabah Cafe (€€€) – Buffet specialising in North-African cuisine. Temporarily working as a Table Service restaurant during Covid-19.
Captain Jack's (€€€€ to €€€€€) – Table Service with international food options. This is inside the *Pirates of the Caribbean* ride building, so you can see the boats sail by as you eat.
Colonel Hathi's Pizza Outpost (€ to €€) – Counter Service with Italian options.
Cool Post (€) – Snacks such as hot dogs, ice creams and crêpes. Plus, hot and cold drinks.
Hakuna Matata (€ to €€) – Counter Service with a constantly changing menu.

Fantasyland

Find classic Disney attractions in this land dedicated to the young and the young at heart.

Disneyland Park's gentle toddler-friendly rides are found here in the most magical of all the lands, and Fantasyland has *plenty* of variety. In addition to the attractions covered in-depth on the following pages, you may also want to visit **The Dragon's Lair** *(La Tanière du Dragon)* and **Sleeping Beauty's Gallery** *(La Galerie de la Belle au Bois Dormant)*. These are both great detailed walk-through attractions inside the park's iconic castle. The Dragon's Lair contains a huge animatronic dragon (more on page 56).

Top Tip: Fantasyland closes one hour before the rest of the park each day to clear the area for the nightly fireworks show.

Peter Pan's Flight

Hop aboard a flying pirate ship and take a voyage through the world of Peter Pan and Never Never Land.

As you soar, you will see scenes to the sides and underneath you, in a retelling of the classic story.

Peter Pan's Flight is one of Disneyland Paris' most popular rides. It features beloved characters, it is family-friendly and provides a small thrill too.

The ride's interior is stunning from the moment you step inside and is truly immersive.

This is an incredibly popular ride so visit the attraction early in the morning, in the evening just before Fantasyland closes, or during the parade.

Yes | None | No | 4 mins | 45 to 75 mins

Important: Visitors who are afraid of heights may want to skip this ride. The ships you sit in make it feel like you'll really flying, and at times you will be several metres off the ground and descending steeply (but not quickly). This may surprise some guests. Mostly, though, it seems to be adults who are affected by this, and not children.

Lancelot's Carousel

No | None | No | 2 mins | Less than 20 mins

This is a beautiful, vintage carousel right in the middle of Fantasyland. It is lined with golden horses, and is a joy to ride for people of all ages.

Waits for this ride are fairly consistent throughout the day but get shorter late in the day and during the daily parade.

Although you can find carousels in almost any theme park, there's something about this one that feels extra magical.

Alice's Curious Labyrinth

No	None	No	10 mins	None

Ever fancied getting lost in the world of *Alice in Wonderland*? Well, now is your chance!

This maze is just challenging enough to keep you guessing where to go next. There are photo opportunities along the way around every corner (or should we say hedge).

Once you reach the end of the maze, you have the option of returning to the park or climbing the Queen of Hearts' castle first. The climb is worth doing for the stunning view over the park. The labyrinth is great family fun and a good way for the little ones to burn some energy.

Meet Mickey Mouse

No	None	Yes	1 to 2 mins	45 to 75 minutes

Mickey is preparing backstage for his next magic show, and you have the chance to meet him. While queuing in the indoor area, you can watch short films playing on a big screen.

Once you reach the front, you will enter a room with Mickey. Here you can meet the big cheese himself, have a chat, and get an autograph and photos.

You are welcome to take your own photos or ask the Cast Member present to help you. Plus, there is a Disney photographer there who will also take an 'official' photo, which you can buy at the attraction's exit.

Note: During Covid-19 you will meet Mickey at a distance, so no hugs sadly - but you can still grab a photo.

Princess Pavilion

No	None	Yes	2 minutes	45 to 90 minutes

Princess Pavilion is your chance to meet one of the Disney princesses. Then chat, play, get an autograph and take some photos.

Outside the attraction, there is a sign that tells you which princesses you will meet at the end of the queue and the time each princess is available for meet and greets.

If seeing a particular princess is a priority, we suggest you visit *Princess Pavilion* as early as possible, as queue lines build up quickly.

Note that queues for this attraction can be long from the start of the day as it typically operates during Extra Magic Time.

"it's a small world" (Closed until late 2022)

"it's a small world" is one of the resort's most memorable and popular attractions, featuring hundreds of dolls singing a catchy song about the uniting of the world.

Guests travel leisurely on boats through scenes representing countries from around the world.

With boats taking lots of passengers, queues are often short. If the wait is longer than 20 minutes, come back later in the day.

Fun Fact

This ride has more audio-animatronics that any other attraction at Disneyland Paris.

No | None | No | 10 mins | Less than 20 mins

This ride is a great Disney classic and is one of the "must-dos" for many visitors.

Blanche Neige et les Sept Nains

No | None | No | 2 mins | 20 to 40 minutes

Relive the tale of *Snow White* for yourself in this classic ride filled with light-hearted scenes, as well as some darker moments too.

Although the ride itself is slow-moving, some moments may scare young children.

The Evil Witch, in particular, makes surprise appearances out of every corner, the dark woods have ominous trees, and thunder and lightning effects may startle younger children.

Mad Hatter's Teacups

Less than 20 minutes | No | 2 minutes | None

Hop inside a teacup and go for a wild spin with the Mad Hatter. This is a theme park classic and great fun for all ages. You can control the spinning by turning the wheel in the centre.

The Adventures of Pinocchio

Ride through a retelling of the story of *Pinocchio* and see the tales from the book and film come to life.

As with the original story, some darker moments may frighten younger children, though these pass by quickly. It is much less frightening than the *Snow White* attraction above, for example.

This ride is not a major attraction like *Peter Pan's Flight*, but it still draws in moderately sized queues due to the popular characters.

No | None | No | 2 mins | 20 to 45 minutes

Sleeping Beauty Castle - *Le Château de la Belle au Bois Dormant*

Standing 51m (167ft) tall, *Le Château de la Belle au Bois Dormant*, is the centrepiece and icon of Disneyland Park.

When the Imagineers were designing Disneyland Park, they knew that the castle here had to be different and unlike the castles in the American Disney theme parks. The European audience was used to seeing real castles, and therefore, the park's icon had to be more fairytale-inspired than real.

The attention to detail is stunning, even including little snails (or *escargots*) on the turrets at the top, and the trees in front of the castle are cut into a square shape just like in the 1959 'Sleeping Beauty' film.

The castle is not just for show, however, and guests can explore it. On the ground floor, you can walk along the drawbridge and over the moat to enjoy this magical building from the inside.

To the right-hand side of the castle, you can see a small wishing well where Disney characters occasionally meet guests - it's a great photo spot.

Behind the castle, you can find the **Sword in the Stone**. Try to remove it if you can, and you could just be crowned king or queen of the kingdom.

Inside the castle, you can enjoy two unique shops, which are incredibly well-themed: enjoy Merlin the Magician's shop on the left, and a year-round Christmas shop on the right.

Once you have completed your shopping, take the winding staircase up to the first floor and see the story of Sleeping Beauty retold using **tapestries** and beautiful **stained-glass windows** in *La Galerie de la Belle au Bois Dormant*. You can even step foot onto the balcony outside for a stunning view over Fantasyland.

The castle's biggest secret, however, is hidden. When looking at the castle from the front, instead of taking the drawbridge, take the path on the left instead. This leads you through a dark passageway and underground into **The Dragon's Lair** *(La Tanière du Dragon)*.

Here you'll find an enormous animatronic dragon (at the time, the biggest ever built) in an area unlike any other Disney theme park around the world. Every few minutes, the dragon comes to life - but don't worry he doesn't breathe fire! You can also access the lair through Merlin's shop.

Dumbo - The Flying Elephant

☆ No | None | 📷 No | 90 seconds | 60 to 90 minutes

Dumbo is one of the most popular rides across the whole of Disneyland Paris.

Located right in the centre of Fantasyland, it offers views of the surrounding area and is a lot of fun.

In front of the seats in each flying elephant, there is a lever that allows you to lift your Dumbo up or down and fly up to 7 metres (23ft) high!

As the ride is popular and has a low capacity, there are long waits all day for this attraction.

Ride it during the parade, during Extra Magic Time, or at the start or end of the day for the shortest waits.

Casey Jr: The Circus Train

Based on the character from Dumbo, Casey Junior is the little circus train that will take you on a ride around models of sets from classic Disney films.

This is a great ride for the whole family. Although it is not a rollercoaster, it can be a good way of seeing whether the kids (or adults) are up to a slightly wilder ride - though this ride is still very tame compared to the other coasters at the parks. Note that adults may feel a bit cramped on this ride with minimal leg and headroom.

There is no height restriction, so everyone can ride, and the low speed is unlikely to frighten anyone.

☆ No | None | 📷 No | 2 mins | 20 to 40 minutes

You will whizz by castles and other story pieces from Disney's classic tales during your ride. For a more leisurely view of these scenes, try the *Storybook Canal Boats* right next door.

Unfortunately, the ride is often closed, or only open for limited periods during the off-season. It also often closes two to three hours before the rest of Fantasyland, so be sure to look out for a sign near the attraction entrance showing if it will close early.

Le Pays des Contes de Fees - Storybook Canal Boats

No | None | No | 5 mins | Less than 20 mins

This is a nice, relaxing ride, where you sail by models of classic childhood tales on a boat.

Along your serene journey, you will see scenes from *The Little Mermaid, Hansel and Gretel, Fantasia, Snow White, The Wizard of Oz* and many more films.

You will even enter the famous cave from *Aladdin*, and see Genie's lamp shining brightly.

It is a nice change of pace from some of the busier attractions in the park, and you can take some great photos of the models.

This is a great attraction for very young children who can look around without anything potentially being scary.

If you want a different perspective on these same scenes, and a faster pace, consider riding *Casey Junior* instead.

This attraction almost always has low wait times, and many people do not seem to know this section of the park exists.

This attraction often closes two to three hours before the rest of Fantasyland and may be closed during the off-season.

Dining

Auberge de Cendrillon (€€€€€) – Table Service (temporarily suspended during COVID-19). This is a restaurant where all the Disney Princesses (and their accompanying princes) roam. They will dance throughout the meal, and visit every table to meet guests too. This meal can be pre-booked and pre-paid as part of a Disneyland Paris package. Breakfast with the Disney Princesses is also available. The only Meal Plan accepted here is the Extra Plus Meal Plan available for arrivals from 31st March 2022.

Au Chalet de la Marionette (€ to €€) – Counter Service with an international menu.

Pizzeria Bella Notte (€ to €€) – Counter Service. Serves pizza, rigatoni pasta and lasagne.

Toad Hall Restaurant (€ to €€) – Counter Service. Serves British fare such as fish and chips, as well as international food such as chicken sandwiches.

The Old Mill (€) – Snack location. Serves crisps, cakes, ice creams, and hot & cold drinks.

Fantasia Gelati (€) – Snack location. Serves Italian-style scoop ice cream and drinks.

Discoveryland

Take a look into the future... from the minds of the past. Discoveryland is inspired by retro-futuristic visions of space and beyond.

Some of the park's most popular and thrilling attractions are located in this land. In addition to the attractions listed below, you can go on a trip around the park from the **Disneyland Railroad's Discoveryland Station**.

Star Wars Hyperspace Mountain: Rebel Mission

Yes | 1.20m | 2 mins | Yes | 45 to 75 minutes

Hyperspace Mountain is a thrilling rollercoaster through space, and it is our favourite coaster at the resort. The beautiful steampunk-style building is the centrepiece of Discoveryland.

Space Mountain is a common fixture at Disney parks around the world but this is the only *Space Mountain* to have inversions and loops, as well as a high-speed launch. It is also the grandest and most extreme of all the *Space Mountain* rides around the world.

At the moment, this ride has a Star Wars overlay so you can expect to see ships from the hit series of films as you soar through space, as well as comets, supernovas, meteorites and other elements from the Star Wars saga, before landing back in Discoveryland. A must-do ride for thrill-seekers!

Top Tip: This ride has a Single Rider queue line, so if you are alone, or do not mind being separated from your party, you can use it to drastically reduce your wait time.

Mickey's PhilharMagic - Discoveryland Theatre

Philharmagic is a fun 4D theatre show for all the family.

The story is that you are attending Goofy's opera performance with Mickey's Philharmonic orchestra. When Donald gets involved, however, things get a little out of hand, and you end up on an adventure travelling through a world of Disney classic movies.

With an air-conditioned theatre, shelter from the rain and a fantastic musical movie, it is easy to see why this attraction is one of our favourites.

Waits are usually non-existent as shows run continuously throughout the day.

Expect scenes and songs from *The Little Mermaid, Coco, Aladdin* and more.

Les Mystères du Nautilus

☆ No	None	📷 No	5 mins	⌛ None

Explore Captain Nemo's ship, the Nautilus, from the Jules Nerve novel *20,000 Leagues under the Sea.*

This incredibly detailed walkthrough takes you under the sea and into the heart of the submarine.

This attraction is a work of art and includes special effects inside such as a giant squid attack, as well as an incredible level of theming and detail.

Kids are unlikely to be entertained, however, as it is a simple walkthrough.

Be aware that some of the noises and effects like the engine room may startle younger members of the family. It is also a bit dark in certain sections inside, but manageable for most people.

Insider Secret: Although you may believe you are inside the Nautilus ship in the lagoon, the winding staircase you use to enter this attraction is designed to disorientate you. Instead of walking towards the ship, you are actually walking down a long corridor and into a show building located between *Autopia* and *Discoveryland Theatre* – the exact opposite direction from the Nautilus.

Autopia

☆ Yes	See notes	📷 No	5 minutes	⌛ 45 to 75 minutes

Hop aboard one of these little cars and take it for a spin around Discoveryland. *Autopia* is hugely popular with kids who get to drive a car for the very first time.

The cars are guided on rails so you can't go too far wrong, but the little ones (and bigger ones also) can steer and accelerate around the track and 'race' others.

The ride is fun, but waits are often long.

Height information: Riders under 0.81m may not ride. Riders between 0.81m and 1.32m must be accompanied by someone over the 1.32m height minimum. Riders over 1.32m may ride alone.

Orbitron: Machines Volantes

☆ Yes	None	📷 No	90 seconds	⌛ 30 to 60 minutes

Soar above Discoveryland in your very own spaceship.

This is a spinning-type ride similar to *Dumbo* in Fantasyland, but the ships here go higher, spin faster and tilt more, making for a surprisingly good thrill.

It is a lot of fun, but it is not a must-do attraction and it is far from unique.

Note: It is a very tight fit for two adults in one spaceship, so avoid this. An adult and a child should fit in a spaceship fine, however.

> A *Star Wars* character meet and greet location called "StarPort" is available in front of *Star Tours* featuring Darth Vador and Kylo Ren.

Star Tours: The Adventures Continue

Star Tours is a 3D simulator-style attraction based on *Star Wars*, but this attraction is equally fun for those who have never seen the films. This is a definite must-do.

In the queue line, you enter an intergalactic spaceport. As you travel through the terminal, you will see Star-Speeders (your transport vehicle), an alien air traffic control station, R2-D2, C3PO, and many robots hard at work to make your journey to space unforgettable.

You will then board your StarSpeeder vehicle for a trip to one of many planets from the *Star Wars* universe.

With over 50 different randomised scenes, you never know what planet you will explore on your ride.

☆ Yes | 1.02m | 5 mins | No | 30 to 60 mins

Most of the dialogue is in French, but it is the visuals and the movement that matter here; the simulator feels incredibly realistic!

Be advised that if you are prone to motion sickness, or dislike confined spaces, you should skip *Star Tours*.

Top Tip: If you want a milder ride, ask to be seated in the front row. This is the centre of the ride vehicle and reduces the movement for riders. For a more thrilling experience, ask for the back row.

Buzz Lightyear Laser Blast

On this interactive ride, you can use laser blasters to shoot at the targets around you to rack up points. Plus, you will be helping Buzz Lightyear defeat the evil Emperor Zurg too.

There are even hidden targets so you can score thousands of bonus points. At the end of the ride, the person with the most points wins. It is competitive, fun and re-rideable – it is also a great family adventure with no minimum height limit.

If you buy an on-ride photo at the end, you can get your scores printed on it too!

☆ Yes | None | Yes | 5 mins | 45 to 75 mins

Top Tip: The highest scoring target is directly in front of Zurg – shoot his medallion repeatedly to get a huge number of points.

Dining
Cafe Hypérion (€ to €€) – Counter Service serving American-style fast food (mainly burgers). In-app mobile orders are available here.

Fireworks

Disney theme parks around the world are renowned for ending visitors' days by lighting up the sky with incredible firework displays. Disneyland Paris is no exception.

Disney Illuminations is Disneyland Paris' dazzling nighttime spectacular which coordinates music, projections, lasers, water fountains and fireworks.

Of all the nighttime spectaculars we have seen at Disney theme parks across the world, *Disney Illuminations* is one of the most impressive.

You can expect to see scenes from *Star Wars, Frozen, Pirates of the Caribbean, The Little Mermaid, The Lion King* and *Finding Nemo*.

Disney Illuminations is performed nightly at the time of Disneyland Park's closing. The show runs for 19 minutes. After the fireworks, Main Street, U.S.A. remains open for about 45 minutes after the park closes for your shopping convenience.

Also, there are other fireworks shows offered on select nights such as Bastille Day and New Year's Eve. On these days, a themed firework display is performed first, followed by *Disney Illuminations*.

Walt Disney Studios Park operates nighttime projection shows on the Hollywood Tower Hotel including during particular seasons such as Christmas. There is also a fireworks display on New Year's Eve (more about seasonal events on pages 90-93).

Lake Disney, by the on-site hotels, offers fireworks on select dates around Bonfire Night and on New Year's Eve too. Admission is free to Lake Disney.

Disney Illuminations Top Tips

1: For the best *Disney Illuminations* spot, we recommend you arrive at least 60 minutes before the show begins. Some guests get spots even earlier than this.

2: Find a spot with a railing in front of you – this prevents someone from turning up during the show and obscuring your view. This often happens when guests put their children on their shoulders as the show begins, ruining the view for everyone behind. Equally frustrating is someone filming the show on their phone.

3: After the show, only Main Street, U.S.A. remains open. There are three main toilet locations for you to use – the first, and the least crowded, is located by the Baby Care Center (Zone J on the map overleaf). The second is inside the arcades running alongside Main Street. The third is at the end of Main Street, U.S.A. and to the right of the *Disneyland Railroad* station at the Arboretum (Zone P).

Disney Illuminations Viewing Guide

Disney Illuminations is primarily a projection show that relies heavily on you having a view of the front of Sleeping Beauty Castle.

Although the fireworks can be seen from across the park, you will miss out on a lot if you are not viewing the front of the castle and its projections.

The front is also where the lasers, fountains and fire effects can be seen.

You will want to position yourself at the central plaza (hub) area of the park or along Main Street, U.S.A. for the best view.

To help you decide on the best view of *Disney Illuminations*, we have created this helpful guide – note that we have invented the zones or areas in the diagram and there are no boundaries between the areas when you are in the park itself.

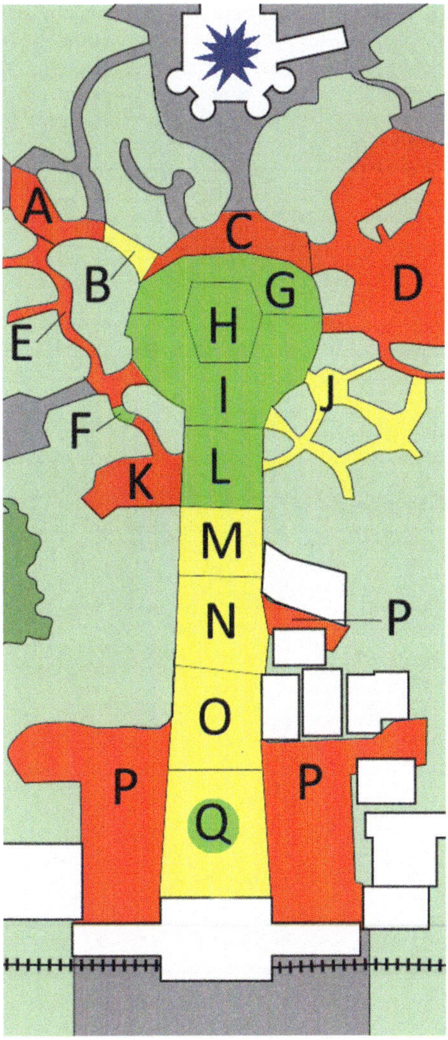

Zone A – A very off-centre view of the show. Not crowded but a last resort.

Zone B – A better view than from Zone A. Uncrowded but this is an off-centre view. Good if you want to see the show last-minute from a decent angle. You may get wet here.

Zone C – Many guests sit or stand here, but this zone is too close to Sleeping Beauty Castle. You will miss some or all of the fireworks behind the castle. The projections do not have their full effect as you will be too close, and you will also likely be sprayed by the water fountains.

Zone D – This area is often cleared by Cast Members and may or may not be open to guests. When the area *is* open, views are not ideal and very off-centre.

Zone E – Views from this area are obstructed by trees, with no visibility.

Zone F – Located off-centre. Behind and to the left of the Disney Illuminations control booth. If you are positioned by the railing here, you will get a fantastic view of the show – this location can only accommodate a few people.

Zone G – This is where guests who arrive early usually wait. This area provides a decent view of the show, and you will see all the fireworks and effects. It is, however, still too close to the action for you to appreciate the show fully, in our opinion. Part of the area on the left of Zone G is reserved for people with disability cards and people accompanying them.

Zone H – Faces the castle head-on and is far back enough to provide a good view of the show. It is not a perfect view but it is very good.

Zone I – Our favourite view of the show. It is the perfect distance from Sleeping Beauty Castle. If you stand by the railings that surround the flowerbeds, you will have a near-perfect view of the show. Be aware of the large speakers and light poles getting in the way.

Zone J – A very off-centre view with many trees meaning poor visibility. This is improved in the winter when there is less foliage and some spots can be decent. When the trees have leaves in warmer months, this is not an acceptable viewing location.

Zone K – Views are obstructed by trees and the *Disney Illuminations* control booth. No visibility.

Zone L – An excellent view; it is a good distance from the castle to see the full show effects while not feeling too distant. This area is also usually less crowded than Zone I. You are also closer to the park exit.

Zone M, N and O – These zones are located along Main Street, U.S.A. and provide an average view of the show. The closer you are to the castle here, the better. These zones are usually less crowded than zones closer to the castle. You will likely see many people in front of you with kids on their shoulders.

Zone P – No visibility.

Zone Q – Must be staked out very early and involves you standing on the bandstand in Town Square – there is very limited space here but it provides an elevated view over other guests on Main street, U.S.A. Specific projections are hard to see from here but the unique view from this location makes it worth considering. We would not recommend this view if you are seeing the show for the first time, however. At the end of the show, you are right by the park exit and well ahead of the crowds.

Parades

Disney Stars on Parade is the best way to see all your favourite Disney characters in one place as they parade through Fantasyland, around the castle hub and down Main Street U.S.A.

The parade is performed daily and the time varies seasonally. Check the in-park Times Guide for the exact schedule.

Characters in the parade may vary from day to day but you can typically see about 50 different characters and floats, including Tinker Bell, Toy Story characters, Simba, Nala, Baloo, Mowgli, Captain Hook, Peter Pan and characters from Finding Dory.

Other characters include Rapunzel, Cinderella, Snow White, Anna and Elsa.

It is not just the characters that are exciting though - the floats are amazing. One of these is a fire-breathing dragon which is sure to take your breath away!

The most popular place to watch the parade is Main Street, U.S.A. You should secure your spot about one hour before the parade starts for the best view if watching from here. At other locations, 30-40 minutes should do.

The parade runs as normal during light or moderate rain. During heavy rain, or if there is a thunderstorm alert, the parade may be cancelled or delayed. In either case, an

announcement is made at the parade start time.

During seasonal events such as Spring, Halloween and Christmas, smaller parades with three to five floats (dubbed cavalcades) are performed several times a day in addition to the main parade.

Walt Disney Studios Park

Walt Disney Studios Park is the second, and newest, theme park at Disneyland Paris. Here you can go behind the scenes and experience the magic of the movies.

Walt Disney Studios Park opened in 2002 and has significantly expanded over the years. In general, the park targets teenagers and adults more than young children and contains several thrill rides. There are also, of course, several attractions for the younger family members.

Despite its expansion over the years, you would still be hard-pressed to spend an entire day in Walt Disney Studios Park due to the limited number of attractions. Disneyland Paris has stated that expanding the park and improving its offerings is a priority.

At the moment, Disney is significantly upgrading the park by adding an *Avengers* area which is due to open in 2022, and a *Frozen* area with a new lake and grand avenue will arrive in 2024.

At 5.3 million visitors per year, Walt Disney Studios Park is Europe's fourth most popular theme park, but still only receives half the number of visitors that its big brother, Disneyland Park, gets next door.

The park is divided into five main areas: Front Lot, Toon Studio, Production Courtyard, Toy Story Playland, Worlds of Pixar, and in summer 2022 Avengers Campus.

COVID-19 CHANGES:
Face coverings are required for guests ages 6 and up at all times at the parks except when eating. Some offerings may be reduced or suspended.

Dining Key:
€ (Under €15)
€€ (€16 to €29)
€€€ (€30 to €39)
€€€€ (€40 to €49)
€€€€€ (€50+)

Prices relate to set menus for one person where available.

All in-park restaurants accept both the Plus Meal Plan and Standard Meal Plan. Learn more about meal plans on page 41.

Front Lot

As you enter the park, you are in Front Lot. This contains the Fantasia fountain as well as a covered area with shops and restaurants.

Front Lot is the entrance area to Walt Disney Studios Park, and home to Disney Studio 1 – an indoor shopping and dining area designed to resemble Hollywood.

Disney Studio 1 is the equivalent of Main Street, U.S.A. in Disneyland Park. The façades of famous Hollywood buildings, as well as all the camera equipment, tell us that this isn't just a recreation, but a 'real' working set designed to be used when making movies.

Sometimes there is street entertainment performed here. This area often offers face painting too (priced at €10 to €14).

Front Lot is home to Studio Services (Guest Services) where you can get assistance, make a complaint, leave positive feedback and apply for disability assistance cards. It is also home to Shutterbugs, the park's photography studio.

Once you have walked through Studio 1, you will see the Partners Statue with Mickey Mouse and Walt Disney holding hands - a great photo opportunity.

Front Lot is also commonly home to photo spots with Disney characters.

Top Tip: If you are dining at *Restaurant En Coulisse*, look up - there is seating on the upper floor, which is open during busier times.

Dining

Restaurant En Coulisse (€ to €€) – Counter Service with American food, mainly burgers. This restaurant is on the right-hand side of Studio 1 behind several façades of famous movie sets.

The Hep Cat Corner (€) – Snacks, serves hot and cold drinks, and ice creams.

Production Courtyard

Stitch Live!

FP: No | Height: None | Photo: No | Duration: 10 minutes | Wait: Until next show

In this interactive theatre show, you'll enter a special transmission room and, before you know it, a Cast Member will connect you and your fellow earthlings to Stitch and you will speak with him live from space.

Stitch is curious about how planet Earth works, so he will ask all sorts of strange questions to learn about our home.

This attraction is good fun. There are separate English and French shows.

The Twilight Zone: Tower of Terror

The Twilight Zone: Tower of Terror transports you to the fifth dimension. You will see incredible special effects and feel what it is like to drop 124 feet (38m).

Disney summarises: "One stormy night long ago, five people stepped through the door of an elevator and into a nightmare. That door is opening once again, and this time it's opening for you."

Star: Yes | Height: 1.02m | Duration: 2 mins | Photo: Yes | Wait: 45 to 75 minutes

You board a service elevator; learn the ghostly past of the hotel, and then you 'drop in'. The elevator is like a free-fall drop ride, except that you are pulled down faster than gravity so you come out of your seat – don't worry, you have seatbelts!

In a split-second, the elevator changes from going up to down, creating a weightless feeling.

The atmosphere inside is immersive and is possibly the best theming at Disneyland Paris. This is a fun ride, but it is an intense experience that WILL have you screaming.

The experience is different inside each elevator so be prepared for a surprise every time you ride.

Cars Road Trip

Star: No | Height: None | Photo: No | Duration: 8 minutes | Wait: 15 to 45 minutes

Hop aboard a studio tram and see scenes from Disney Pixar's hit film *Cars*.

You'll see the biggest lugnut in the world, experience 'Cars-tastrophe Canyon', see Mater's junkyard creations including an Eiffel Tower made of car parts and more.

This is a short but fun family adventure for all ages.

An older version of this attraction was called *Studio Tram Tour: Behind the Magic*.

The Disney Junior Dream Factory at Studio D

Launched in 2021, this new shows how powerful dreams are.

You can expect to see Vampirina, Timon, Mickey, Minnie and 'Fancy' Nancy Clancy bring the stage to life with fun songs.

The show lasts about 25 minutes.

Toon Studio and Worlds of Pixar

Crush's Coaster

Crush's Coaster is a unique attraction and the only of its kind in any Disney theme park worldwide.

Guests board turtle shells in groups of four, sat back-to-back in pairs. The first few scenes are a slow-moving dark ride but then you reach the rollercoaster portion where you spin as you ride the waves with Crush.

Although the ride may seem to target younger kids, do not be fooled - this is a wild, fast adventure, so read the warning signs outside first.

The popularity of the characters and the ride's low capacity means this ride regularly has the second-longest queue in the park, after *Ratatouille*. Even on less busy days, queues exceed 40 minutes and it is common to see a wait time of over 90 minutes.

Ride *Crush's Coaster* first thing in the morning or just before park closing for the shortest waits.

In the last hour before park closing, a long wait time is often displayed to discourage people from getting in the queue line.

Top Tip: The wait time for the Single Rider queue is often exaggerated to avoid waits getting too long.

Top Tip

While waiting in the queue, connect to the local Wi-Fi network from any smartphone to play a unique Crush touchscreen game.

No	1.07m	No	2 mins	90 to 120 mins

Frozen Animation Celebration

No	None	No	30 minutes	Until Next Show

This attraction is a mix of shows, meet and greets and other experiences themed to *Frozen*.

Guests move between three different rooms - the first is themed to a log cabin with Anna and Sven joined by Elsa.

Then, you'll move to Elsa's Ice Palace for a sing-along.

At the end, you will find Olaf who you can meet and get photos with.

Flying Carpets over Agrabah

No	None	No	90 seconds	Less than 30 minutes

Board one of Aladdin's flying carpets and fly over Agrabah. As you soar through the skies, you will hear the Genie through his director's megaphone telling you how to act.

The ride itself is a simple spinner ride, and is very similar to both *Dumbo* and *Orbitron* (at Disneyland Park) – this ride, however, often has shorter queues.

Here you can raise and lower your carpet, and tilt it backwards and forwards!

Cars Quatre Roues Rallye

No	None	90 secs	No	15 to 45 minutes

Hop in for a spin on Route 66 with the characters from Disney Pixar's *Cars*.

The ride is similar to the teacups ride in Disneyland Park, but you spin faster and in different directions in this version.

Vehicles can accommodate up to 2 adults, plus 2 extra kids.

Animagique Theater – "Mickey and the Magician"

No	None	No	30 minutes	Shows at set times

Note: This show is currently suspended during Covid-19 and the theatre is being as a character selfie spot, but we expect this show to return in 2022.

Go back in time to Paris at the turn of the 19th century... and enter a great Magician's workshop, where the assistant is none other than Mickey Mouse!

As well as the main cheese himself, you will see Tinker Bell from *Peter Pan*, Lumière from *Beauty and the Beast*, Genie from *Aladdin*, the Fairy Godmother from *Cinderella*, Rafiki from *The Lion King*, and even Elsa from *Frozen*.

With unforgettable songs such as "Let it Go" and "Friend like Me", this is an unmissable spectacular. We think this is one of the best shows that Disneyland Paris has ever done - it is of West End theatre quality.

Ratatouille: The Adventure

Board a 'ratmobile' and travel through the streets of Paris, scurrying along rooftops and kitchens in a clever 4D immersive ride.

Yes	1.02m	5 mins	No	45 to 75 minutes

Along your journey, your 3D glasses and giant screens put you in the heart of the action. Feel the heat from a grill, the chill of a refrigerator, and you may even get splashed once or twice. There are also different smells throughout.

Ratatouille vehicles do not follow a track, taking slightly different paths for a unique experience each time.

This ride often has one of the longest waits in both theme parks. In the last hour of park operation, an inflated wait time is often displayed to discourage people from queuing.

A Single Rider Line is available. This typically reduces wait times to less than 30 minutes and often to less than 15 minutes. On busy days, waits in this queue can reach 60 minutes.

RC Racer

Hop on the RC car from Pixar's *Toy Story* films, and feel the wind in your hair as you ride both forwards and backwards along the track.

The ride is great fun and a good adrenaline rush – it is often compared to the swinging pirate ships found at many theme parks. However, here you are also secured by overhead harnesses.

At the highest point, riders are 24m (80ft) up, and the free-fall-like feeling backwards is great fun.

The ride looks more intimidating than it actually is, in our opinion.

RC Racer has one of the most slow-moving and tedious queues in all the park so we would avoid it if waits are long.

No | 1.20m | No | 2 mins | 45 to 75 mins

Top Tip: A Single Rider queue is available for guests to save time and board individually. Unfortunately, this Single Rider queue only starts halfway into the regular queue so you may have to wait in the normal queue line for a long time until the split point.

Ride this early in the day as queues build up quickly.

Toy Soldiers Parachute Drop

Board one of the Toy Soldiers' parachutes and get ready to soar up into the sky and then glide back down to the ground again and again.

This is a great fun family ride.

No | 0.81m | No | 1 min | 45 to 75 mins

Queues can get extremely long for this ride, so get here early.

Top Tip: A Single Rider queue line is available for guests happy to board individually.

Slinky Dog Zigzag Spin

Hop on *Slinky Dog* and enjoy yourself as you spin round and round in circles getting increasingly faster and faster.

This is a fun family-friendly attraction that will entertain everyone from young toddlers to parents.

No | None | No | 90 secs | 20 to 45 mins

Dining

Bistrot Chez Remy (€€€ to €€€€€) – Table Service. Set menus only. Advanced reservations are recommended as this is the only Table Service restaurant in the park.

Avengers Campus

This new area of the park will open in Summer 2022. In addition to the below attractions, you can also expect a character meet and greet area.

Iron Man: Jukebox

This is a high-speed rollercoaster that is replacing the old Aerosmith-themed *Rock n' Roller Coaster* with an *Iron Man*-themed version.

On this coaster, guests will team up with Iron Man, Captain America and other superheroes. You'll reach speeds of 92 km/h (57 mph) and can expect to go upside down several times on this ride.

Yes | 1.22m | Yes | 90 secs | 90 to 120 mins

Expect long waits for this attraction when this new land opens.

The image shown here is concept art.

Web Slingers: A Spider-Man Adventure

This is the family-friendly attraction in this new land.

In this interactive ride, you'll use your hands to sling webs onto screens to catch the Spider Bots.

The ride recently opened in California and it is a fun family-friendly attraction but is not mind-blowing.

As a new ride, expect long queues after opening.

Yes | None | No | 4 mins | 120 to 150 mins

Parades and Fireworks at Walt Disney Studios Park

Live entertainment at Walt Disney Studios Park is limited to the stage show *Mickey and the Magician*, as well as seasonal entertainment. Unfortunately, this park does not have a daytime or nighttime parade, nor does it have a regularly scheduled nighttime show or fireworks. You will find the nightly fireworks show at Disneyland Park.

Exceptions: There is a firework show offered for guests at this park for the transition from New Year's Eve to New Year's Day at midnight. During *Season of the Force* and the Christmas Season, there is a nighttime spectacular projected onto *The Twilight Zone: Tower of Terror*'s building façades.

Touring Plans

Touring plans are easy-to-follow guides that minimise your wait time in queue lines throughout the day. By following them, you can make the most of your time in the parks and experience more attractions. There are several different touring plans available to suit your needs.

To see all of Disneyland Park, you will need to allocate at least two days. However, you can hit the headline attractions at the park in just one day if you are pressed for time. Walt Disney Studios Park can be comfortably seen in one day.

Unless you are visiting during an off-peak season, you will find it difficult to see the highlights from both parks in one day – there is not enough time.

These touring plans are not set in stone, so feel free to adapt them to the needs of your party. It is important to note that these plans focus on experiencing the rides; if your focus is on meeting all the characters or seeing all the shows, then a touring plan is unlikely to be suitable for you. The only way to minimise waits for characters is to get to the parks (and meet and greets) early.

These touring plans are intense, BUT you will get to see and do as much as possible during your visit. If you are at the resort for multiple days, feel free to follow the plans at a more leisurely pace. Also, if you do not want to experience a particular ride, skip that step but do not change the order of the steps.

If an attraction is closed for refurbishment during your trip, skip the respective step.

You must purchase your tickets in advance to make the most of your time and these touring plans. If you need to buy a ticket on the day, turn up at least 30 minutes earlier than the recommended start times on these plans - and even earlier during peak season.

Insider Tip: To minimise the time you spend waiting in queue lines, you will often need to cross the park from one side to the other. Note, for example, how the three roller coasters at Disneyland Park are all in different lands and far away from each other – this is purposely done to spread crowds more evenly.

Disneyland Park Touring Notes

Two attractions that are not covered in these plans:

• *Thunder Mesa Riverboat Landing* - The wait time for this attraction is never longer than 30 minutes (and typically around 15 minutes) so you may be able to fit it in.

• *Disneyland Railroad* goes around the park. There are four different stations to board at, but the one with the shortest waits is usually Frontierland Station as it is the most hidden away.

Be aware that both these attractions stop operation well before the park closes.

Disneyland Paris also lists the following as attractions, so you might want to fit them in at some point:

• *Horse-Drawn Streetcars*
• *Main Street Vehicles*
• *The Liberty* and *Discovery Arcades*

We do not feel these are must-dos unless you have time to spare.

This guide does not take into account live shows, as those vary throughout the year, check your Times Guide for more. Be sure to watch them.

Also, be sure to visit the *Gallery* inside Sleeping Beauty Castle (upstairs) and the *Dragon's Lair* underneath. Entry to Sleeping Beauty Castle ceases at least one hour before *Disney Illuminations*, as does all of Fantasyland.

Disneyland Park

1 Day Plan for Guests with Extra Magic Time

Step 1: At 8:15am be at the park gates for entry - the park opens at 8:30am. Make sure you have downloaded the Disneyland Paris app. This lists parade, show, character and firework times, as well as attraction closures. If you want to meet any characters, do this now, before the rides. Walk down Main Street, U.S.A., get photos and head straight to *Sleeping Beauty Castle*.

Step 2: Enter Fantasyland and ride *Dumbo: The Flying Elephant* first, followed by *Peter Pan's Flight*.

Step 3: Head to Frontierland and ride *Big Thunder Mountain*.

Step 4: If it is not yet 9:30am, ride *Phantom Manor*. If it is 9:30am or later, enter Discoveryland and ride *Buzz Lightyear Laser Blast*.

Step 5: Ride *Orbitron - Machines Volantes*.

Step 6: The park should now be open to all guests. Ride *Autopia*.

Step 7: Ride *Star Wars Hyperspace Mountain*.

Step 8: Ride *Star Tours: L'Aventure Continue*.

Step 9: Visit *Les Mystères du Nautilus.*

Step 10. Time to visit Fantasyland. Here ride *Les Voyages de Pinocchio* and *Blanche Neige et les Sept Nains*.

Step 11: Grab some lunch.

Step 12: You now have a few rides left to do in Fantasyland. Experience *Casey Junior, Le Pays des Contes de Fées, "it's a small world"* (closed until late 2022) and *Le Carousel de Lancelot*. Ride these one after another, in any order you wish, if you want to do them all. *Casey Junior* and *Storybook* close several hours before the rest of the park.

Step 13: If any live shows such as *The Lion King* are playing during your visit, you may want to watch these now.

Step 14: Check the time of the parade, and grab a spot at least 45 minutes before the start time.

Step 15: Many guests leave the park after the parade, so it will now be less busy. This is the time to either take a bit of a rest on a bench to avoid burning out or to go on rides that have fast-moving queues. Ride *Pirates of the Caribbean*.

Step 16: Ride *Indiana Jones et le Temple du Péril.*

Step 17: Now depending on what time of the day it is, and when the park closes, it is either time to have dinner or do the walkthrough attractions.

Walkthrough attractions do not have a waiting time. These include *Adventure Isle and La Cabane des Robinson, Le Passage Enchanté d'Aladdin* and *Alice's Curious Labyrinth*.

Step 18: Grab a spot for *Disney Illuminations* at least 45 minutes before showtime. We like to grab a hot dog and fries from *Casey's Corner* and eat this while waiting for the show to begin.

1 Day Plan for Guests without Extra Magic Time - Focus: Kids Rides

Step 1: Arrive at 9:20am at Disneyland Park's entrance. Enter the park when it pre-opens at 9:30am. Until 10:00am you can shop, eat and ride the *Main Street Vehicles*. Make sure you have downloaded the Disneyland Paris app. This contains parade, show, character and firework times, as well as attraction closures and park hours.

Step 2: Walk down *Main Street, U.S.A.*, get photos and proceed straight to *Sleeping Beauty Castle.*

At *Sleeping Beauty Castle*'s hub lies the entrance to all the lands of the park – Disney Hotel guests and some annual passholders will have access to the rest of the park at this time.

Stand by the rope leading to the castle and Fantasyland. This rope is removed at 10:00am so all guests can go through.

Step 3: Ride *Peter Pan's Flight.*

Step 4: Ride *Dumbo the Flying Elephant.*

Step 5: Ride *Autopia.*

Step 6: Ride *Buzz Lightyear Laser Blast.*

Step 7: Have lunch.

Step 8: Ride *Casey Junior.*

Step 9: Ride *Le Pays des Contes de Fees* next.

Step 10: Ride *Pinocchio,* and *Snow White's Scary Adventures* in Fantasyland.

Step 11: Get a spot for the parade at least 45 minutes before the start time anywhere along the parade route. Check the app for the start time.

Step 12: Explore inside *Sleeping Beauty Castle.*

Step 13: Ride *"it's a small world"* in Fantasyland (closed until late 2022).

Step 14: Decision: *Explore Alice's Curious Labyrinth* or ride *Le Carousel de Lancelot*. If there is still a lot of time left until the park closes, do both.

Step 15: If any shows are playing, now is a great time to watch one.

Step 16: Ride *Pirates of the Caribbean* in Adventureland.

Step 17: Ride *Phantom Manor* in Frontierland.

Step 18: Have dinner.

Step 19: Grab a spot for *Disney Illuminations* at least 45 minutes before showtime. We like to grab a hot dog and fries from *Casey's Corner* and eat this while waiting for the show to begin.

Note: If your children want a thrill, *Big Thunder Mountain* in Frontierland should be your choice, as it does not go upside down and is the tamest roller coaster in the park.

1 Day Plan for Guests without Extra Magic Time - Focus: Thrills

Step 1: Arrive at 9:20am at the entrance to Disneyland Park. Enter as the park pre-opens at 9:30am. Until 10:00am you can shop and eat on Main Street, U.S.A. and ride the Main Street Vehicles. Make sure you have downloaded the Disneyland Paris app. This contains parade, show, character meeting and firework times, as well as attraction closures and park hours.

Step 2: Walk down Main Street, U.S.A., get photos and proceed straight to *Sleeping Beauty Castle*.

At *Sleeping Beauty Castle*'s hub lies the entrance to all the lands of the park – Disney Hotel guests and some annual passholders will have access to the rest of the park at this time.

Stand by the rope leading to Frontierland. This rope is removed at 10:00am so all guests can go through.

Step 3: Ride *Big Thunder Mountain* in Frontierland immediately when the park opens.

Step 4: Ride *Star Wars Hyperspace Mountain* in Discoveryland.

Step 5: Ride *Star Tours*.

Step 6: Ride *Indiana Jones et le Temple du Péril* in Adventureland. Now you have ridden all the roller coasters in this park.

Step 7: Ride *Pirates of the Caribbean*.

Step 8: Time for lunch.

Step 9: If you are interested in watching any shows such as *The Lion King*, now is a perfect time.

Step 10: Explore *Les Mystères de Nautilus* and other walkthroughs such as *Le Passage Enchanté d'Aladdin* or *La Cabane des Robinson*.

Step 11: Ride *"it's a small world"* (closed until late 2022).

Step 12: Get a spot for the parade at least 45 minutes before the start time anywhere along the parade route. Check the app for parade timings.

Step 13: Ride *Autopia*.

Step 14: Ride *Phantom Manor*.

Step 15: Ride *Peter Pan's Flight* and explore *Alice's Curious Labyrinth*.

Step 16: Have dinner.

Step 17: Grab a spot for *Disney Illuminations* at least 45 minutes before showtime. We like to grab a hot dog and fries from *Casey's Corner* and eat this while waiting for the show to begin.

2 Day Disneyland Park Touring Plan

If you want to experience everything Disneyland Park has on offer in two days, follow the 1-Day plan for 'Kids Rides' on one day, followed by the 1-Day plan for 'Thrill Rides' the next day. This will cover all the rides in the most logical sequence. Combine the touring plans with Extra Magic Time if you have that available to you and you should be able to comfortably experience Disneyland Park and all its attractions.

If you have three days or longer at Disneyland Park, there is no need to follow our touring plans rigidly. Make sure to arrive early, and visit the busiest rides at the start or end of the day.

Walt Disney Studios Park

Important: If you are visiting after Avenger's Campus opens in summer 2022, first ride *Web Slingers: A Spider-Man Adventure* followed by *Iron-Man: Jukebox*. Then, follow the touring plan below.

Important 2: Guests with Extra Magic Time access should ride *Crush's Coaster* first, followed by *Ratatouille* (if Avenger's Campus is open ride *Crush* first, then *Spider-Man*, then *Iron Man* and lastly *Ratatouille*)

Step 1: Arrive at the Walt Disney Studios Park entrance by 9:20am. Enter the park at 9:30am when it pre-opens. Make sure you have downloaded the Disneyland Paris app before your visit. Walk through *Studio 1* briskly - you can come back and look around this area later.

Step 2: Ride *Crush's Coaster*.

Step 3: Ride *Ratatouille: The Adventure*.

Step 4: Visit Toy Story Playland. There are several attractions to experience here. Ride them in this order: *Toy Soldiers Parachute Drop*, *RC Racer* and *Slinky Dog*.

Step 5: Ride *Cars Quatre Roues Rallye* – this is located opposite *Crush's Coaster*.

Step 6: Ride *The Twilight Zone: Tower of Terror*.

Step 7: Get a standby pass for *Crush's Coaster*.

Step 8: Experience *Animation Celebration* - check the schedule in your app.

Step 9: Ride *Cars Road Trip*.

Step 10: Ride *Flying Carpets over Agrabah*.

Step 11: Watch some of the park's shows.

Step 12: That is it for all the rides. This park is tiny in comparison to Disneyland Park.

As well as the character meets (during Covid-19 these are replaced with selfie spots), there are three main shows left to experience, so take these in according to their schedules which are available in the app.

These shows are:
- *Stitch Live*
- *Mickey & The Magician*
- *Disney Junior Dream Factory*

Outside the Parks

A trip to Disneyland Paris isn't just about the theme parks - there are a wealth of things to do outside the parks such as the shopping district, Disney Village. Plus, the fun does not have to stop at the resort. After all, you are just outside one of Europe's largest and most vibrant cities. Plus, there are opportunities for shopping and other adventures nearby.

Disney Village

Disney Village is an entertainment district located just next to the theme parks and on-site hotels where you can continue the fun after the parks close. This area houses a cinema, restaurants, shops, bars and more. Admission to Disney Village is free.

Entertainment

Panoramagique

Soar into the sky and get a bird's-eye view of Disneyland Paris from the world's largest helium-filled passenger balloon – *Panoramagique*.

This is a great way to take some photos of the resort where you can see everything around you, including both theme parks, Disney Village and the resort hotels.

It truly is a unique perspective from where you can appreciate all the different activities on offer at the resort.

Pricing is €15 per adult and €8 per child for the flight (free for children under 3). A meal deal which includes a flight on *Panoramagique* and a meal at *Earl of Sandwich* is also available.

Flights last 6 minutes and do not operate in periods of high wind, or adverse weather conditions.

La Marina

La Marina offers water activities from rowing boats to pedal boats, and electric boats to hydro bikes. Land-based activities are also available such as surrey bikes which you can hire. Activities operate at a charge and are based on weather conditions.

Operating times are 16:00 to 22:00 daily during high season (school holidays) and on weekends. Activities may also be available at other times.

Pricing:
- *Electric boat hire* – €20 for 20 minutes, 5 people maximum per boat
- *Hydro Bikes* – €5 for 20 minutes, 1 person per bike. Minimum age: 12.
- *Pedal Boats* – €10 for 20 minutes, 5 people maximum per boat.
- *Surrey bike* – €10 for 20 minutes for a 2-adult + 1 child bike, or €15 for 20 minutes for a 4-adult + 1 child bike.

More Entertainment

- **Disney Stadium** - In between the Disney Store and the Sports Bar, the Disney Stadium is a tiny hole-in-the-wall location where you can play classic arcade-style video games, as well as air hockey. Games are mostly priced at €2 each.
- **Sports Bar** - Being at Disneyland Paris does not mean missing out on your favourite sporting events. Go to *Sports Bar* and watch the game on the huge screen, while having a drink or two and a snack. *Sports Bar* also hosts weekly karaoke sessions and other forms of live entertainment open to everyone at no cost.
- **Billy Bob's** - As well as being a restaurant during the day, *Billy Bob's* is a bar and nightclub when the night draws in. Children are allowed in at all times of the day and night, except during some adult-only events. Cast Members often frequent the bar at the end of a hard day's work at the theme parks – here drinks are free-flowing and adults and children alike can dance the night away.
- **Cinema Gaumont** - With 15 different auditoriums, including one with an IMAX screen, there is bound to be something for you to enjoy watching at this cinema. You can check film schedules in advance at http://bit.ly/dlpcinema. Films listed as VOST (usually only one) are shown in their original language with French subtitles.

Dining

Dining Key:
€ (Under €15)
€€ (€16 to €29)
€€€ (€30 to €39)
€€€€ (€40 to €49)
€€€€€ (€50+)

Prices relate to set menus for one person where available.

Most restaurants at Disney Village do not accept Meal Plans unless otherwise stated.
EPMP = Accepts Extra Plus Meal Plan only.

Disney Village has a variety of dining options, from Quick Service (fast food) to Character Dining options (Disney characters visit each table while you eat) to more traditional Table Service restaurants (order from a menu and your food is served by a waiter).

McDonald's (€)– Counter Service. *McDonald's* is a well-known fast-food chain, but this branch has higher prices than usual due to the location. A standard meal costs between €8 and €9, with a child's meal costing about €5. Be aware that queues can be long if you do not use the automated terminals and want to order from an actual employee instead. The terminals can be set to English easily and accept bank cards but not cash; we highly recommend using these.

Starbucks Coffee (€) – Counter Service. This is a standard *Starbucks* location. However, it should be noted that *Starbucks* is not cheap in France, and this location is no exception. A hot or cold brewed drink is priced between €4 and €6, and sandwiches are about €5.

Earl of Sandwich (€) –

Counter Service. Prices are about €7 for a "gourmet" heated sandwich and €8 for a salad. The adult sandwich set menu is €11.50, with a kids' set menu at €7.50.

An "Adult Balloon Flight" meal is available and includes a warm sandwich, crisps, a soft drink or bottle of water, a chocolate brownie or cookie, and one flight on *Panoramagique*. A "Child Balloon Flight" meal includes a mini-sandwich, a soft drink or bottle of water, a mini chocolate brownie or fruit cup, and one flight aboard *Panoramagique*.

Cafe Mickey (€€€€) [EPMP] – Table Service. Usually a character dining restaurant but not during COVID-19. Characters are currently set to return in late March 2022 if the pandemic allows.

Annette's Diner (€€ to €€€) [Accepts all meal plans] – Table Service. The American-style breakfast menu is €15. Milkshakes are €11 to €12.

King Ludwig's Castle (€€)– Table Service. Here there is a special lunch menu (dish of the day style) served until 5:00pm. Dinner options are set menus or a la carte.

Planet Hollywood (€€€) – Table Service. No adult set menus. Main courses are €15 to €33. The kids' set menu is €12.50.

Rainforest Cafe (€€ to €€€)– Table Service with a unique rainforest-like ambience. Main courses are €19 to €32.

The Steakhouse [PLMP, PRMP] (€€ to €€€€) – Table Service.

New York Style Sandwiches (€) – Quick Service and snack location. Serves sandwiches, hot and cold drinks, and ice creams.

Billy Bob's Country Western Saloon – Billy Bob's is divided into two dining establishments – **Bar Snacks** (€), a snack and Quick Service location, and **La Grange** (€€€) [Accepts all meal plans], an all-you-can-eat Tex Mex buffet.

Sports Bar (€) – Counter Service and Snacks. Snacks are served until 11:00pm. Sandwiches, burgers, pasta bolognese, hot dogs and fish and chips and pizzas.

Vapiano (€) – Counter service. Amazingly fresh food. Pick a seat, then order your pizza or pasta from a food station, it's made fresh in front of you in minutes — our favourite fast food location in Disney Village. No set menus; main courses are €11 to €14.

Five Guys (€) – Counter service. The best burgers at Disneyland Paris, in our opinion. Expect to pay €7 to €12 for a burger. Fries and drinks are extra.

Shopping

After a meal, you may want to treat yourself to a little bit of retail therapy; here you are spoilt for choice with several merchandise locations.

World of Disney – As you walk into Disney Village from the parks, this is the first store you see. *World Of Disney* is the best place to get your Disney merchandise outside of the theme parks. It is also the largest store at the resort, featuring a beautiful interior, plenty of tills to pay at, and a good selection of merchandise.

The Disney Store – This classic location is a traditional-style Disney store. Uniquely, here you can create your own lightsabers, and your own Potato Head figure, as well as purchase from a selection of more common Disney merchandise.

Planet Hollywood Store – Get items with the *Planet Hollywood* brand on them. This store mainly stocks apparel.

The Disney Gallery – This location features collector's items such as figurines and paintings. Also, you can take advantage of *Disney's Art on Demand* kiosks, where you can order a print from an interactive display. This poster is then created and delivered to your home. With over 200 different posters to choose from, there is something for everyone.

LEGO Store – This is the largest LEGO store in France. It features all kinds of different LEGO sets, but unfortunately, it does not feature any exclusive Disney-themed merchandise. Nevertheless, it is worth a visit for fans of the colourful bricks.

Disney Fashion – Love a Disney shirt or hoodie? This is your haven.

World of Toys – This store is the place to buy princess dresses, dolls, and sweets.

Rainforest Café Store – The perfect place to get all your *Rainforest Café* branded merchandise.

Paris

Disneyland Paris is located a mere 35 minutes away from the centre of Paris by train, so visiting the 'City of Lights' should be considered on an extended trip.

Paris is filled with monuments, museums, rich culture and history. You should try to visit some of the following world-class attractions during your time in the city such as the Eiffel Tower, Musée du Louvre, Musée d'Orsay, Arc de Triomphe, Champs Elysées, Montmartre and the Sacre Coeur church.

Museums are generally reasonably priced, and European Economic Area citizens (the UK is not included) aged under 26 get free entry to most museums in the city. Plus, non-EEA visitors under the age of 18 get free entry with ID. There are even monthly openings of the museums with free admission for everyone, regardless of age.

We recommend taking a cruise on the river Seine or a bus tour, which will allow you to see several monuments in one go.

If you wish to visit several attractions and get unlimited public transport, the Paris Pass is worth considering.

To get to central Paris, catch the RER A line train from *Marne-la-Vallee – Chessy* station, located just a two-minute walk from the parks. Once you are in the centre of Paris, you may need to use the metro to get to various destinations.

A Mobilis day pass is the best travel ticket (priced at €17.80 for zones 1 to 5). It allows unlimited travel for one day until midnight on the transport system within the Paris region, including to and from Disneyland Paris.

Disneyland Paris sells several excursions to Paris:

Paris Essentials – A free-style tour with time to explore alone. It includes a return coach trip from Disneyland Paris and a river cruise in Paris. Prices are €49 per adult and €39 per child. The tour runs between 10:15am and 7:45pm (8:30pm in summer).

Versailles & Paris Tour – Return coach transport from Disneyland Paris, entry to Versailles Palace, transfer to city centre, and a river cruise. Prices are €117 per adult and €84 per child. This tour departs at 10:00am and returns at 8:30pm.

Other tour options are also available from €69 per person.

Val d'Europe

Located minutes away from Disneyland Paris is *Val d'Europe* - a town designed by Disney with a huge shopping centre and outlet mall.

It is only one stop away from Disney on the RER A line train (€1.95 per journey). Trains run every 10 minutes with a journey time of about 2 minutes.

Alternatively, you can catch the number 50 hotel shuttle bus which is free from just outside *Marne la Vallée - Chessy* train station.

If you are taking the bus, you will exit at the last stop by the *Hotel l'Elysée*. Cross the road at the pedestrian crossing and the shopping centre is in front of you. These buses run somewhat infrequently during the day.

If using the RER train, make sure to leave *Val d'Europe* station through the exits marked *Centre Commercial*.

Outside the station, turn right and walk straight ahead, crossing the road. The shopping centre will be in front of you. Note that it is closed on some public holidays. Shops are open from 10:00am until 9:00pm on Monday to Saturday (and close at 8:00pm on Sunday), with restaurants staying open until midnight daily.

If you would like to stock up on groceries, there is a huge supermarket in the shopping centre, as well as a SeaLife aquarium (entry is €16 to €20 per person), and hundreds of stores.

You can also follow the signs to *La Vallée Village* outlets for designer luxury goods at reduced prices.

Villages Nature

Villages Nature is a partnership between Disneyland Paris and Pierre et Vacances. It is located 15 minutes from the main Disneyland Paris site and accessible by a (paid) public bus service.

This new eco-tourism location has been built around a geothermal lagoon. It features apartment-style accommodation, numerous restaurants to enjoy and recreation options.

A shuttle bus runs between *Villages Nature* and Disneyland Paris, and you can book accommodation packages to stay at Villages Nature and play at Disneyland Paris.

The *Aqualagon* (an indoor water park) features giant water slides, a wave pool, and an outdoor lagoon heated to 30 degrees Celcius year-round. This is open daily from 10:00am to 8:45pm.

Also on offer: *BelleVie Farm* hosts educational programs and workshops; *Extraordinary Gardens* is a set of four landscaped gardens inspired by the four elements; *Forest of Legends* is a huge outdoor playground; Tree-climbing trails; a bowling alley; boutiques; cultural events and much more.

If you are not staying at the accommodation, you can buy a day pass to visit this unique location for €35 to €50 per adult and €20 to €40 per child. On certain days you can also buy a half-day pass which allows access from 5:00pm to 11:00pm for €25 per adult and €15 per child. Parking is an extra €10. Book at centerparcs.eu/in-en/villages-nature-paris-day.

Accommodation starts at €391 for 2 nights.

Davy Crockett's Adventure

If you like adventure assault courses, you will love *Davy Crockett's Adventure*! There are swings, trapezes, rope bridges, ladders and much more for you to explore, making this High Rope location great family fun.

This attraction is located at the entrance to *Disney Davy Crockett Ranch* – a campsite run by Disneyland Paris and considered one of the seven on-site hotels. It is 8km from the central resort hub.

This activity is open seasonally – visit www.aventure-aventure.com (French only) for opening times (Under 'Préparer ma visite' and then 'Calandrier'). The assault courses are operated by a third-party company and not Disneyland Paris.

Note there is no shuttle bus to *Disney Davy Crockett Ranch* where this activity is located. You will need a car if you wish to participate in the experience, or you can book a taxi or use the public bus number 47 from *Marne-la-Vallée Chessy* bus station (paid).

Guests with Disabilities

Disneyland Paris is designed to be enjoyed by everyone, regardless of their mental or physical abilities and over 60,000 guests with disabilities visit each year.

Accessibility Cards

If you have a guest with an officially-recognised disability in your party, stop by the Disney Hotels front desks or the dedicated desks at the entrance to either park on the first day of your visit. Alternatively, you can start the process in advance online at bit.ly/prioritydlp.

If you have visited Disneyland Paris, please note this system was overhauled in December 2021.

Guests who have a disability can apply for one of two cards that will facilitate their visit: the Priority Card and the Easy Access Card.

Both cards have a photo of the holder as well as a QR code to confirm validity.

The **Priority Card** allows a permanently disabled guest and up to 4 members of their party access to attractions via a specially adapted entrance. This entrance will involve less walking and no stairs. It could be through the ride's exit, through the Disney Premier Access entrance or a specially adapted queue line. In cases that the standard queue line is adapted, you will use the standard access. Entry procedures vary from ride to ride – to learn the boarding options available to you at each attraction, ask a Cast Member at the ride entrance.

This card provides priority but not instant access; wait times vary based on the number of people in the Priority Card queue. To receive the card, the disabled person (or their helper) must present an official document issued by the local government or medical authorities from any country. A medical certificate will not be sufficient. Proof of ID is required and may be requested when boarding rides.

Valid supporting documentation to prove disability varies greatly between countries and we recommend checking bit.ly/prioritydlp for the full list.

The **Easy Access Card** is for guests with a recognised Long Term Chronic Disease. The full list of 30 eligible illnesses can be seen at bit.ly/easyaccessdlp. Examples vary from a debilitating stroke to diabetes, and leprosy to cystic fibrosis.

You'll need an original medical certificate in French or English signed and stamped by a medical doctor and less than 3 months old, indicating the long term chronic disease.

This card can only be obtained at Disneyland Paris and not in advance - you can do this at Guest Services at the entrance to the parks or at your hotel's front desk.

This card does not offer priority access. Instead, you will present the card at an attraction entrance, receive a time-slot reservation to return and then can enter the ride at that time bypassing the regular queue line. You can only make one ride reservation at a time.

This card is valid for the named guest plus up to 4 members of their party.

Additional information: When a disabled person asks for a Priority Card, they are asked questions to determine which rides will be accessible to them. For example, someone who cannot transfer out of a wheelchair may not ride Pirates of the Caribbean.

As well as the card itself, you will be given a copy of the Accessibility Guide with detailed information on each attraction. You can also consult this in advance at www.bit.ly/dlpdisab before your trip.

Some attractions require that guests with either card make a reservation at the ride entrance and return later. Organised character meet-and-greets usually use a reservation system, and there will be a Cast Member with the characters to reserve a slot for you.

Some attractions may not be accessible to guests with certain disabilities. In this case, family members cannot use the card in place of the disabled person – they must use the standby queue or can pay for Disney Premier Access, if available.

Expectant mothers can get a bracelet that acts similarly to the Easy Access Card at their Disney hotel or Guest Relations at either park. A medical certificate dated within the last 3 months in English or French is required. You can be accompanied by 4 people for the attractions and shows, and 2 people for the parades.

Services for Guests with Disabilities

Hearing-impaired visitors: Disney Park information points, as well as some Walt Disney Studios Park attractions, are equipped with induction loops to assist guests. These *attractions are CinéMagique Theatre, Animagique Theatre, The Disney Junior Dream Factor, Stitch Live!* and *The Twilight Zone: Tower of Terror*.

Mobility impaired visitors: Cast Members cannot escort or help disabled guests to attractions. They will, of course, provide directions and assist inside attractions.

Some attractions require that disabled guests transfer from their wheelchair to an attraction vehicle. For these attractions, disabled guests must be accompanied by at least one non-disabled adult (18+) to assist. Cast Members may not help visitors in or out of their wheelchair or ride vehicles. For some attractions, visitors must be ambulatory.

In Walt Disney Studios Park, all attraction queues are wheelchair accessible; this is also the case for *Buzz Lightyear Laser Blast, Princess Pavilion* and *Meet Mickey Mouse* in Disneyland Park. For attractions where this is not the case, a Priority Card allows guests entry via a separate entrance.

Designated viewing areas are available for guests in wheelchairs for the daily parade, *Disney Illuminations* and stage shows.

All toilets have accessible areas for visitors with reduced mobility.

Unisex toilets (with cubicles so a carer may join wheelchair users) are available in every land of Disneyland Park.

All shops and Table Service restaurants are accessible. At Quick Service places, ask a Cast Member for assistance if necessary.

An accessible shuttle bus is available between all Disney hotels (except *Disney's Davy Crockett Ranch)* and the theme parks. Ask at the hotel desk, the Disney Express desk in *Marne La Vallée – Chessy* station, or Guest Services in the parks for details and to book this free service.

Disney Hotels each have rooms adapted to meet the needs of guests in wheelchairs. These have an extra-large bathroom with a bath, handrails and a raised toilet. Additionally, mobility-impaired guests can hire a seat to help them to wash without assistance (to be requested when making the reservation).

The bedroom door has a spy hole at wheelchair height in accessible rooms. Bathrooms at *Disney's Davy Crockett Ranch, Sequoia Lodge* and *Santa Fe* Hotels have a shower suitable for mobility-impaired guests.

Visually impaired guests:
An app called AudioSpot available on both iOS and Android describes surroundings, attractions, and food menus in audio form.

In some areas of the park, a companion may need to describe the surroundings. Some attractions and areas of the park are dimly lit.

At hotels, Disney recommends that visually impaired guests inform the hotel reception of their visual impairment upon arrival. A Cast Member will show guests to their room, and show them around the rest of the Disney hotel so that visually impaired guests can orientate themselves.

Telephones and TV remotes with large buttons, as well as room keys with Braille, may be requested when making a reservation or at reception upon arrival.

Guide Dogs:
Guide and assistant dogs are allowed in the parks and on certain attractions. On attractions where dogs are not permitted, they must be left with a helper. Dogs may not be left unattended or with a Cast Member. Visually impaired guests may need to be accompanied on certain attractions. If bringing a guide dog, there must be at least two helpers with a disabled guest – one to accompany the guest, and another to stay with the guide dog.

Food Allergies:
Disneyland Paris offers allergen-free meals at selected restaurants. We recommend warning your hotel so an allergen-free breakfast can be prepared. When booking Table Service meals, state your allergies. Review Disneyland Paris' allergen guide at www.bit.ly/dlpallergy.

Other information:
Cast Members may refuse guests access to attractions for safety reasons.

Some attractions only accept one disabled guest at a time for safety and legal reasons. In these cases, the wait for a disabled guest can be as long or longer than the standard queue line.

Guests with medication that must be kept cool may leave this at one of the First Aid points in the two theme parks or Disney Village.

For safety reasons, all visitors: with reduced mobility or visual impairment, with a cognitive or mental health disorder, with a behavioural disorder or autism or with a learning disability, are recommended to be accompanied by at least one non-disabled companion over the age of 18 to assist them. This is not compulsory but Disneyland Paris recommends this for a guest's first visit.

Some attractions may have low-light areas, flashing lights or loud sound effects, dropping floors and other effects. Companions should pay particular attention to all these factors when preparing for the stay and should read the safety information available at the entrance to each attraction, as well as the Disney Parks Accessibility Guide.

Ticket discounts:
Guests with a disability (as well as one accompanying person) are entitled to a 25% discount on park tickets and annual passes.

An official document issued by your local government or medical authorities from any country will be accepted as proof of disability. A medical certificate will not be sufficient.

These tickets can be purchased at a Disney hotel or the park entrances at dedicated desks.

Disneyland Paris for Walt Disney World Regulars

Many guests visit Disneyland Paris after having visited the Walt Disney World Resort in Florida. Both resorts immerse you in the Disney magic, but it is important to understand that the two locations are very different. This chapter helps you compare and contrast.

The Cast Members and Languages

The Cast Members in Florida and California, for the most part, go above and beyond, are incredibly polite, have a passion for Disney and do everything to make your stay as magical as possible.

However, the Cast Members in the US are restricted by the Disney rulebook, which even affects their personal lives such as how they can cut and style their hair.

Disneyland Paris is a Disney Park for the 21st century in a country where a 'Disney Look' dictating employees personal appearance is illegal. French employment laws are stringent, so Cast Members cannot be reprimanded for not smiling or for leaning at work.

Also, French customer service is very different from that in the USA. Having said this, most of the Disneyland Paris Cast Members are pleasant, inviting and helpful – just do not expect American-style customer service in France.

All Cast Members must speak at least two major European languages, one of which must be French.

Almost all the entire Cast speak English well, but it is not mandatory. You may, on a rare occasion, encounter a Cast Member that does not speak English, so it pays to learn some basic French.

It is basic manners to learn some of the language when visiting another country and at least say *Bonjour* and *Merci*.

Weather

Florida is known as the "sunshine state", and you can expect daily high temperatures to reach 30°C (80-90°F) for much of the year - especially in the summer. There are occasions where there are cold snaps and the temperature drops for a few days, but nothing to the levels seen in Paris.

Paris' weather is much more variable; the average daily temperature in Paris in July and August is about 25°C (77°F) whereas temperatures in January and February are 3°C (37°F) on average, often dipping below freezing. In the summer, it is common for a few days to exceed 37°C (100°F) in Paris.

Visitors to Walt Disney World have to deal with Hurricane season much of the year (June to November) when the weather can be extreme, and hurricanes are possible. These are not usual in Paris.

Orlando visitors also deal with a tropical climate with daily thunderstorms in the summer, closing all outdoor attractions and drenching anyone not prepared. Paris' rain is more unpredictable and is present year-round but thunderstorms are rare.

Local Customs

According to the latest available figures from Disneyland Paris, before the pandemic, 48% of all visitors to the resort were French, and 16% were from the UK. Other countries with a high number of guests include Spain and Italy. Disneyland Paris has a very high proportion of European visitors, unlike Walt Disney World.

Many American customs do not apply to a European audience. For example, many Europeans do not queue in daily life. Instead, people gather in small groups instead of an orderly queue. So, when a bus arrives, it is a free-for-all and people rush for the doors with no regard for those who have been waiting for the longest.

During random character appearances in the parks, you can expect a crowd of parents pushing their children to get their photos taken first. When a queue is set up, though, Europeans do comply.

Tipping is also different. Meals in France have a service charge included in the price so there is no need to tip (although a small tip is appreciated). This compares to the US, where tips of 15% or 20% of a meal's price are expected.

In general, guests are less respectful at the Parisian parks – they enter cordoned-off areas, sit anywhere they want, and smoke in the parks despite it being banned in most areas.

Guests in Europe also often expect to have an alcoholic beverage with their meal – as such, you will find beer on sale at Quick Service locations. Wine and other alcoholic drinks are also offered at all Table Service locations. The sale of alcoholic drinks has *not* harmed the parks' family-friendly atmosphere.

Lastly, the European audience is a little bit more fashion-conscious than the crowds that visit Florida. Ponchos, for example, are sold at Disneyland Paris, but they are often replaced by umbrellas and raincoats in Europe instead. Having said this, there is more than a fair share of guests dressed "interestingly" at Disneyland Paris.

Resort Size and Transportation

The size difference between the two resorts is staggering: Walt Disney World is 40 square miles or 103 square kilometres. In comparison, Disneyland Paris is 22.3 square kilometres.

From the furthest resort hotels to the parks is a 20-minute walk at Disneyland Paris or a 5-minute bus journey. However, at Walt Disney World most journeys cannot be walked - not only because of the distance but because there are no pavements connecting most areas due to the resort's sprawling size and American car dependency.

At Disneyland Paris, the two theme parks are within

walking distance, as is the Disney Village. Everything is a bus journey away from each other at Walt Disney World.

The advantage of Disneyland Paris' small size is that you can walk across the whole resort, you can visit the other hotels easily, and you spend less time travelling and more time enjoying yourself. The disadvantage is that there are fewer things to do: no water parks, fewer hotels, and crucially fewer theme parks (there are two in Paris, versus four in Florida).

Looking at the theme parks, Disneyland Park is slightly bigger than Magic Kingdom Park, but with emptier, quieter areas and fewer rides. Park walkways feel much less crowded in Paris.

Walt Disney Studios Park in Paris is about half the size of Disney's Hollywood Studios in Orlando. The resort hotels in Paris are also generally smaller than their Floridian counterparts.

In fact, Disneyland Paris is much more comparable to Disneyland Resort in California where everything is within walking distance. Paris' resort is still *much* larger than the Disneyland Resort, however.

The area where Disneyland Paris is located is as much a major transport hub, as it is a world-class theme park resort.Just two minutes from the park entrances, you can hop on a high-speed train to travel across France, or even to the UK.

Alternatively, you can use the regional trains and travel into central Paris in just 35 minutes. You can also drive and be at non-Disney locations in just a few minutes too.

Disneyland Paris is all very self-contained, so if you do fancy escaping the magic, it is easy to do - unlike in Florida! For some people, this is a benefit, though others prefer the Floridian immersion of the Disney magic that lets them forget about the outside world.

Pricing

Disney trips can be very pricey. At Disneyland Paris, room prices at on-site hotels include tickets to the theme parks for the length of stay. However, you will not find a room at a Disney hotel for under €250 per night for 2 people – and these are the cheapest rooms during off-peak seasons.

In contrast, the cheapest hotels in Walt Disney World are half this price, though park tickets are not included. At Disneyland Paris, there are almost always special offers available, so you shouldn't be paying the full rate.

A one-day entry ticket to Disneyland Paris for one park is €99 (£83 or $113) for adults and €80 for children. A two-park ticket is €119 (£100 or $135) and €111 respectively. The daily rate drastically reduces the longer you visit the resort. A 4-day ticket is €259 (£217 or $295) for adults. You can get significantly discounted tickets online, however.

For comparison, at Walt Disney World, a one day, one park adult ticket is $116 to $169 with tax, or a park hopper (for four theme parks) is $185 to $238. A 4-day ticket is $435-$597 for one park per day, or $525-$687 with the park hopper option).

Walt Disney World tickets are substantially more expensive. Although there are more activities in the Floridian parks, the 4-day hopper costs twice as much per person.

Longer stays of 7 or 14-days at Walt Disney World become more affordable per day.

Food prices at Disneyland Paris are slightly more expensive in comparison to the US and many people bring picnic food into the parks for this reason.

A burger, fries and drink combo will set you back about €15 (£13/$18) at Disneyland Paris. A burger

and fries in the US will set you back about $12 without a drink, or about $16 with one. With tax, the price is actually around the same at $17.

At Table Service establishments, the price difference is more notable, however they are still close. A Set Menu at a good in-park restaurant will set you back €50 to €60 ($60 to $72) at Disneyland Paris. The equivalent at Walt Disney World would be about 30% cheaper, but you then need to add on a tip and tax.

Food-wise don't expect signature foods like Dole Whips and Mickey Premium Bars in Disneyland Paris, either - or snacks in general, as snacking is less of a European concept.

Skip-the-line systems

At Disneyland Paris, if you want to skip the standby queues at rides, you can use Disney Premier Access and pay for every ride.

At Walt Disney World, you can pay $15 a day to skip the queue at many rides at each park with Genie+. However, the top 2 rides in each park are not included in this and are an extra fee just like Paris' Disney Premier Access system.

Both systems are digital and are run on a smartphone.

The previously free Fastpass system no longer exists at either resort.

Unique Attractions and Details

Disneyland Paris has many unique rides and shows which cannot be found at Walt Disney World.

In Disneyland Park, *Phantom Manor* is a beautiful reimagining of the classic *Haunted Mansion* ride with a new storyline and an entirely different interior but keeping many familiar scenes.

Pirates of the Caribbean is much longer, has a better queue, new scenes and bigger drops in Paris.

Star Wars Hyperspace Mountain is beautiful in Paris - it is an intense looping roller coaster that blows the other Space Mountains out of the water; *Big Thunder Mountain* is more intense and fun in Paris, and is set in the middle of an island.

Furthermore, there are lots of unique walkthroughs such as *The Nautilus* and *Alice's Curious Labyrinth* too. *Casey Junior* and *Storybook Canal Boats* also do not exist in Florida.

Indiana Jones et le Temple du Peril is also a unique roller coaster. There is, however, no 'New Fantasyland expansion' in Paris.

The *Disney Illuminations* night-time spectacular is not too dissimilar to Magic Kingdom's *Disney Enchantment*.

In Walt Disney Studios Park, *Crush's Coaster* is a unique spinning roller Coaster in the dark, and *Cars Quatre Roues Rallye* is a tea-cup style ride themed to Cars. *Cars Road Trip* is unique too.

Toy Story Playland has three unique rides, and *Animagique Theatre* is home to a unique stage show. *Stitch Live* is a cool interactive show, similar to *Turtle Talk with Crush*.

Finally, the new Avenger's Campus coming in summer 2022 will feature a brand new Iron Man rollercoaster, as well as an interactive Spider-Man ride that Florida does not have.

Disneyland Park is beautiful. Everything is incredibly elaborately themed, sharing inspiration from the US parks while introducing unique elements that cannot be found elsewhere.

In comparison, the theming in Walt Disney Studios Park is still sparse and leaves a lot to be desired.

Although over the past five years there has been an effort to improve the park, Walt Disney Studios Park lacks the detail that makes Disney theme parks unique.

Even Disney's Hollywood Studios, which is (in our opinion) the worst-themed park at Walt Disney World, has superior theming to the Studios park in Paris. The Avengers Campus expansion will help but it is the future *Frozen* and *Star Wars lands* that will really improve this park.

The hotels at Disneyland Paris are American-themed but do not live up to the resort hotels found at Walt Disney World. The hotels in Paris are just hotels, whereas you could spend several days at the hotel resorts in the US and enjoy the surroundings and experiences on offer.

The Seasons and The Future

Disneyland Paris offers its guests something different throughout the year, with seasonal and special events that celebrate traditions such as St. Patrick's Day, Halloween and Christmas. This section explores all of these. Plus, we take a look at the future of the resort.

St. David's Welsh Festival

Early March. May return in 2022 subject to Covid-19.

This three-day-long mini-season has traditionally been celebrated in Frontierland, at Disneyland Park.

During the festival, guests can take photos with some of their favourite Disney characters clad in traditional Welsh robes.

Also, Disneyland Paris usually has traditional Welsh singers, such as a choir, perform at the festival several times throughout the day.

Traditional music, a crafts market, traditional food and drink, complimentary face painting, and a special St. David's fireworks display make the festival a fun and unique event.

St. Patrick's Day

17th March. May return in 2022 subject to Covid-19.

Much like the St. David's Day celebrations above, this one-day celebration of all things Celtic takes place in Frontierland, at Disneyland Park.

Guests can enjoy live traditional music, photo opportunities, character appearances, a pre-parade, and a special St. Patrick's Day fireworks display.

Disneyland Paris Pride

11th June 2022

Celebrate the magic of diversity and show your pride with this after-hours event at Disneyland Paris.

The event will feature an exclusive parade, live performances by famous artists, the chance to ride some of our most popular attractions late into the night, appearances by favourite Disney characters and much more.

Disneyland Paris MagicRun Weekend

Late September. Cancelled in 2021. May return in 2022.

This event includes several races designed to test your stamina.

- **5km Run** – A 5km run from 8:00pm. Ages 5 and up.

- **Kids Races** – Kids races for children under 12. There are 100m, 200m and 1km races.

- **10km Run** – This 10km run will take place exclusively inside Disneyland Paris grounds with characters en-route.

- **Half Marathon** – The main 21.1km half-marathon starts at 7:00am. It goes through both theme parks, hotels, as well as the local villages around the theme parks. Disney characters are stationed throughout the route. The Half Marathon race is open to ages 18+ only and a medical certificate is required.

- **RunDisney Health & Fitness Expo** – Daily in the Disney Events Arena. Here participants can get their race T-shirt, race number bib and gear bags. Plus, everyone can see the latest in fitness apparel, footwear, sunglasses, gadgets, and nutritional products.

The Expo includes a Speaker Series with appearances by celebrity runners and seminars on training, running, and nutrition featuring speakers and panellists from the running industry.

Race participants receive a medal for each race completed and refreshments during and after their race. Special medals are available for those who complete multiple races.

Travel package bookings are available which include hotel stays, park tickets and race entry.

Race-only prices for the last event were: €77 for the half-marathon, €60 for the 10km, €43 for the 5km and €16 for the kids run. 2022 prices will likely be a few euros more if the event goes ahead.

Disney's Halloween Festival

October and early November

Disneyland Paris' Halloween season is one of the most elaborate celebrations at the resort, with unique shows, parades, décors and more to delight guests.

This information is for 2021's Halloween season as it is too far to know what the season in 2022 will look like. Some events may not return for the 2022 season, and new events may be added, but this sets expectations as Halloween is broadly similar each year.

Disney usually releases specific details about six weeks before the season starts.

Stage Show – See the Disney Villains out in full force in this show on the Royal Castle Stage. This was suspended in 2021 but we expect it to return in 2022.

Decorations, Food and Merchandise – Frontierland is invaded by ghostly decorations for some great photo opportunities. Disney characters also sport Halloween-themed costumes. Villains-themed merchandise and special Halloween-inspired menus are available.

Character Meets – Keep your eyes peeled for meet and greets with Disney characters in their Halloween best.

Mickey's Halloween Celebration Parade – Treat yourself to Mickey's tricks as he steals the show on a fabulous Phantom Manor float in the wickedly wonderful Halloween Cavalcade. Souls of all ages will get in the spirit as Disney Characters parade along the streets of Disneyland Park in eye-popping autumn attire. You're sure to be spellbound!

Disney's Halloween Party (2021 info):
On 31st October between 8:00pm and 2:00am, this ticketed event offers an evening of frightening entertainment.

Most Disneyland Park attractions are open during

the event and guests may wear Halloween costumes (subject to restrictions).

Entry is €79 for guests aged 3 and up. Under 3s go free. Guests may enter from 5:00pm with party tickets.

Unique entertainment is available during the party including character meet and greets, special shows and lots of exclusive party-only entertainment.

Mickey's Magical Fireworks and Bonfire

Early November

See the night sky transformed above Lake Disney as Disney sets its fireworks off to music to celebrate Bonfire Night. The show lasts about 20 minutes.

Lake Disney is in front of the on-site Disney hotels - no park entry is required and admission is free.

Christmas

Mid-November to early January

For the most magical time of the year, make Disneyland Paris your stop. Here you are guaranteed snow every day, magical characters and unforgettable experiences.

The following details are for the 2021 Christmas season. Traditionally, the Christmas seasons do not change hugely from year to year so you can expect much of this information to be valid for the 2022 Christmas season too. Information on the 2022 season will not be unveiled by Disney before September 2022 at the earliest.

The park will be filled with Christmas touches everywhere you go but no more so than Main Street, U.S.A - here you will find a giant Christmas tree, snowmen on each corner and baubles and tinsel abound.

Show: A Fairy Tale Waltz with Disney Princesses – Get your twinkle toes over to Royal Castle Stage in Disneyland Park for the Starlit Princess Waltz – a magical Christmas ball thrown by Disney royalty. Watch as the biggest ever gathering of Disney royal couples - including Belle, Cinderella and Aurora - whirl, twirl and unfurl majestically around the dance floor.

This show was not performed in 2021 but a similar show usually plays each year outside of the pandemic.

Mickey's Dazzling Christmas Parade – This Christmas-themed parade marches down Fantasyland and Main Street, U.S.A. The parade stars Father Christmas until Christmas day. The regular parade, *Disney Stars on Parade* is also usually performed once daily during the Christmas season.

Mickey's Magical Christmas Lights – Every evening as the night falls, the park's signature Christmas tree comes to life with the help of Mickey, Minnie and Santa in this illumination ceremony. The show takes place every evening.

Meet Characters – You can meet both Santa and Mickey at *Meet Mickey Mouse*. There are two queue lines – one for Mickey photos and the other for Santa photos. You'll also have the chance to meet Marie from the Aristocats, Scrooge McDuck, Thumper, Miss Bunny and more throughout the park!

Special Dinners – In Europe, Christmas Eve and New Year's Eve dinners are a big family affair. As such, dinners on these days are available for a heavy supplement.

Prices vary from €129 to €259 per adult on Christmas Eve. On Christmas day a special 4-course lunch is available for about €180 per adult. New Year's Eve meals range in price from €119 to €299 per adult.

Full details on these meals are available over the phone and on the Disneyland Paris website.

We think these prices are extortionate, with a family of 4 spending at least €400 on a single meal. Our recommendation is to eat at one of the Quick Service restaurants to avoid these hefty price tags (or at a Table Service location as a late lunch).

Alternatively, choose from one of the Table Service restaurants not offerings special dinners, or eat at Disney Village at selected restaurants. Reservations are strongly recommended.

New Year's Eve

31st December

Celebrate the start of the New Year at Disneyland Paris.

This is traditionally the busiest day at the resort and you can expect the theme parks to reach maximum capacity with very long wait times for all rides.

If you can put up with that, you can experience a fireworks display at Walt Disney Studios Park or Lake Disney (no admission cost at this last location).

Walt Disney Studios is open until 1:00am meaning you have one hour of post-fireworks attraction time.

All the Christmas entertainment is still running on this date and continues into early January.

Disneyland Park is not open past 7:00pm to regular day-guests, as it has a paid party. See below.

New Year's Eve Party: Disneyland Paris promises a star-studded evening packed with surprises. Enjoy the incredible New Year's Eve Parade. Above *Sleeping Beauty Castle*, the New Year fireworks will amaze, and why not take to the dance floor or enjoy a whole host of other surprises?

This is a ticketed party - tickets are €109 per guest and allow entry from 5:00pm to 1:00am - the park is open for ticket holders only starting from 7:00pm. The party typically sells out well in advance.

The Future - Projects in Progress & Rumours

Walt Disney Studios Park Expansion – Walt Disney Studios Park is set to continue to expand in size, and with additional attractions - Disney is investing €2 Billion into the theme park in total.

Construction has already started and the project is expected to open in phases from 2022 until 2025.

The three new areas coming to the park are:

• Avengers Campus includes a new Iron Man roller-coaster (opening 2022), a Spider-Man interactive ride (opening 2022), and a Marvel character meet and greet.
• Frozen area with a new ride (opening 2024-2025)
• Star Wars area with one new ride (rumours say this may be cancelled due to the impact of COVID-19)

Disney says: "In addition to the three new areas, the creative vision includes a new lake, which will be the focal point for entertainment experiences and will also connect each of the new park areas."

Disney Village Expansion – Disney Village is set to be expanded over the coming years, with new shopping and dining experiences.

Hotels – Disneyland Paris has been refurbishing all of its hotels over the past decade. The Disneyland Hotel is currently closed for a complete overhaul.

Plus, there are plans for a new "value"-priced on-site hotel. Construction has not started on this, so this is still many years off.

A Special Thanks

Thank you very much for reading our travel guide. We hope this book has made a big difference to your trip to Disneyland Paris, and that you have found some tips that will save you time, money and hassle! Remember to take this guide with you when you are visiting the resort. This guide is also available in a digital format.

If you have any feedback about this guide, or have noticed changes in the parks that differ from what is in the book, do let us know by sending us a message. To contact us, visit our website at www.independentguidebooks.com. You can also sign up for our newsletter there for information on new releases.

If you enjoyed this guide, we would love for you to leave us a review wherever you purchased this guide from. Your reviews make a huge difference in helping other people find this guide. Thank you and have a magical time!

If you have enjoyed this guide, other travel guides in this series include:

- The Independent Guide to Walt Disney World
- The Independent Guide to Universal Orlando
- The Independent Guide to Universal Studios Hollywood
- The Independent Guide to Disneyland
- The Independent Guide to Hong Kong Disneyland
- The Independent Guide to Shanghai Disneyland
- The Independent Guide to Tokyo Disney Resort
- The Independent Guide to Universal Studios Japan

Photo credits:
The following photos have been used from Flickr (unless otherwise stated) in this guide under a Creative Commons license. Thank you to: Disneyland Hotel (cover) - Edgardo W. Olivera; Tower of Terror (cover) - David Jafra; Eurostar (small) - 'kismihok; Eurostar (large) - Philip Sheldrake; Thunder Mesa Riverboat, Blanche Neige and La Cabane des Robinson, Newport bay close, Dumbo, Phantom Manor, Indiana Jones, Peter Pan, it's a small world, Wild West Show - Loren Javier; Dumbo & Pinocchio - Jeremy Thompson; Nautilus - Paul Beattie; Star Tours - Anna Fox; and Ratatouille exterior - Eleazar; Fastpass (single) - Joel; Fastpass (multiple) - JJ Merelo; View of Lake Disney (La Marina section) - Nicola; Val d'Europe - Tves Jalabert; Davy Crockett's Adventure - aventure-aventure.com; Golf - DisneylandParis.com; Aerial Image - Apple Maps; Disney Dollars - R Reeves; Teacups - Kabayanmark Images; Newport Bay far - Nicola; New York Hotel - .Martin.; Crush parade float - Moto@Club4AG; Sleeping Beauty Castle - Sergey Galyonkin; BTM and Halloween- Kevin Marshall; Tower of Terror - Ken Lund; Ratatouille - Martin Lewison; Parachute Drop - Ludovic; Panoramagique - Victor R Ruiz; Eiffel Tower - Pedro Szekely;.

Disneyland Park Map

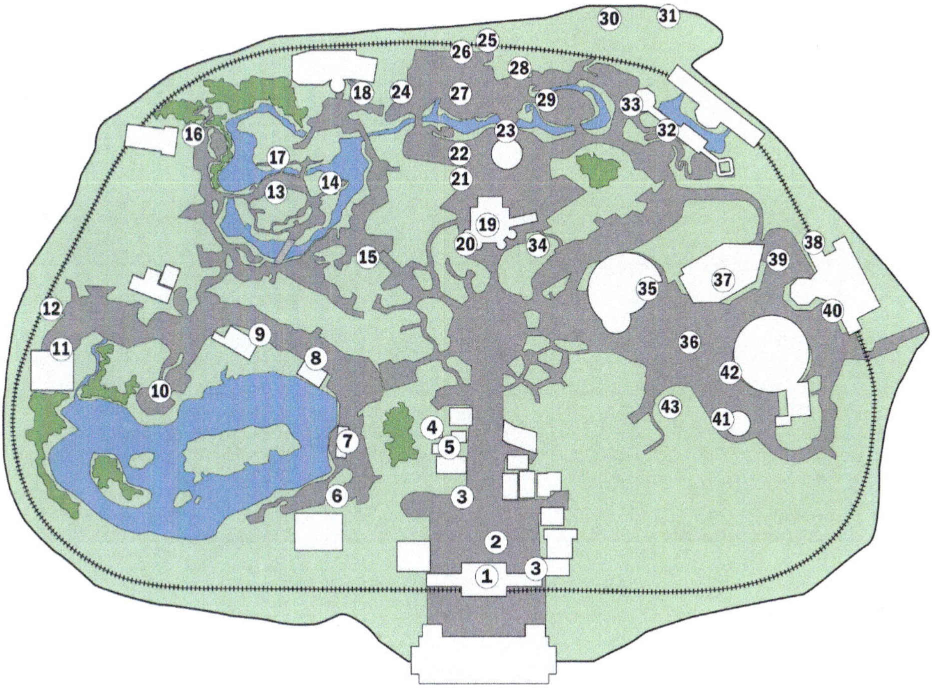

MAIN STREET, U.S.A.
1 - Main Street, U.S.A. Station
2 - Horse-Drawn Streetcars
3 - Main Street Vehicles
4 - Liberty Arcade (Statue of Liberty Tableau)
5 - Dapper Dan's Hair Cuts

FRONTIERLAND
6 - Phantom Manor
7 - Thunder Mesa Riverboat Landing
8 - Rustler Roundup Shooting Gallery (extra charge)
9 - Big Thunder Mountain
10 - Pocahontas Indian Village
11 - Frontierland Theatre (Lion King: Rhythms of the Pride Lands)
12 - Frontierland Station

ADVENTURELAND
13 - La Cabane des Robinson (Treehouse)
14 - Pirates' Beach
15 - Le Passage Enchanté d'Aladdin
16 - Indiana Jones et le Temple du Péril
17 - Adventure Isle
18 - Pirates of the Caribbean

FANTASYLAND
19 - Sleeping Beauty Castle
20 - Dragon's Lair
21 - Snow White and the Seven Dwarfs
22 - Pinocchio's Fantastic Journey
23 - Le Carrousel de Lancelot
24 - Peter Pan's Flight
25 - Fantasyland Station
26 - Meet Mickey
27 - Dumbo: The Flying Elephant
28 - Alice's Curious Labyrinth
29 - Mad Hatter's Tea Cups
30 - Casey Jr. - le Petit Train du Cirque
31 - Storybook Canal Boats/Le Pays des Contes de Fées
32 - "it's a small world"
33 - Princess Pavilion
34 - Castle Stage

DISCOVERYLAND
35 - Buzz Lightyear Laser Blast
36 - Orbitron
37 - Videopolis
38 - Discoveryland Station
39 - Star Tours
40 - Discoveryland Theatre
41 - Les Mystères du Nautilus
42 - Star Wars Hyperspace Mountain
43 - Autopia

Walt Disney Studios Park Map

FRONT LOT
1 - Disney Studio 1

PRODUCTION COURTYARD
2 - CineMagique Theatre
3 - Animagique Theatre
4 - The Twilight Zone: Tower of Terror
5 - Studio D: The Disney Junior Dream Factory
6 - Stitch Live!

TOON STUDIO AND WORLDS OF PIXAR
7 - Frozen: A Musical Invitation
8 - Flying Carpets over Agrabah
9 - Crush's Coaster
10 - Cars Race Rallye
11 - Cars Road Trip
12 - Ratatouille: The Adventure

TOY STORY PLAYLAND
13 - Toy Soldiers Parachute Drop
14 - Slinky Dog Zig Zag Spin
15 - RC Racer

AVENGERS CAMPUS
16 - Web Slingers: A Spider-Man Adventure
17 - Iron Man: Jukebox Rollercoaster

Printed in Great Britain
by Amazon

81359223R00059